This story is based on actual events. Certain characters have been changed and entirely fictitious. Any resemblance to real persons, living or dead, is purely coincidental.

Copyright Ⓒ 2014 by Mohamed Ammouri

Dedication

I dedicate this book to my daughter Layan, my son Walid and all the young Palestinians everywhere, to keep the dream alive, and honor the memory of all those who gave their lives for Palestine.

Table of Content

Chapter 1

Roots and History

I was born in a place where turmoil was created and nourished almost every day. Rebellion was deeply rooted within the psychological structure of Palestinians in Lebanon, especially those in the refugee camps. The belief of being a victim, living with the great purpose of correcting injustice, was mixed with almost every function of daily living.

Understanding my background and belonging started very early in my life, a child with a single-digit age, looking at the world through the eyes of my family, who, just a few years before, lost a good way of life which parents, grandparents, most of the extended family members, even neighbors and friends, talked about continuously. Their life was in a place which provided an abundance of love and prosperity; a place to where I traveled in my imagination to escape the harsh reality of everyday life in a place where I was born, but have no deep connection with.

I thought living in Lebanon was just temporary, not what should've been. It felt just like a bad dream, or just really a tough time for me and my family. I thought it would end soon after, then I would find myself, along with my parents, brothers, sisters, relatives, even neighbors and school friends, all back in the homeland . . . the place where happiness once existed . . . and life would continue from where my family left off and left behind a home and a country.

Acre the Hometown

My father was a well-known men's custom tailor. He owned a shop, a house, a car, which was not very common at the time, and even owned a couple of land lots. On one he planned to build a big house for the family. My grandfather was a chief fisherman. Their hometown was Acre, more than two thousand years old, a historic city extending its land into the Mediterranean Sea. My family was very happy in that place. Most of my family members kept talking about it. The wall surrounding the old city of Acre once made it impossible for Napoleon Bonaparte to defeat the city after a long siege. He had to turn away from it. Even though Napoleon occupied most of the countries in the area, he still could not invade the old city of Acre people of the city and some books say. Napoleon settled for throwing his hat above the city wall into the city as some symbol of achievement before he left. Maybe it was a symbol of respect for a worthy enemy who put up a good fight. That old city was a fortress, and continued to look like one, even to this day.

Inside the city, old souks, markets, were covered by arched ceilings above all the shops, where shoppers took their time without having to worry about rain or too much heat from the sun. The old city had a famous Turkish bath, where men and women took turns to enjoy it, and an old prison which housed many famous leaders, including leaders of the Palestinian rebellion against the British Mandate during which they ruled Palestine for over 20 years.

A castle stood there, a clock tower attached to an ancient traveling merchants' hostel, and the prominent Jazzar Mosque, built by, and named after, the famous ruler of Acre. He was appointed by the Ottoman sultan. He was feared for his firm, decisive, and ruthless ways of ruling, but he was also admired for his courage to lead the city to stand up and face Napoleon's army.

Acre was also known to have produced Ahmad al-Shuqayri, the founder of the Palestine Liberation Organization, "PLO." Al-Shuqayri was a distant relative of my family. While still a child, I often heard my father and other family members mention his name when they discussed politics of Palestine.

Acre was like a painting being drawn piece by piece in my mind until it became complete. I could walk its streets in my imagination and see all those places I was told stories about. Acre became my virtual hometown.

Palestine

A country of a little over 27,000 square kilometers, it borders Egypt, the Mediterranean Sea, the Red

Sea, the Dead Sea, Jordan, Syria, and Lebanon. It holds a very rich history of peoples and different civilizations, which goes back thousands of years. Their presence can be seen through historic ruins, castles, and religious symbols, including the walls which surround ancient cities like Jerusalem, Jaffa, and Acre, the land most known to the rest of the world as the "Holy Land." It is where Abraham and his descendants resided. A shrine in Hebron hosts their tombs. Jesus Christ was born in Bethlehem, spread his message, and was crucified in this land. His tomb lies in the heart of Jerusalem. Prophet Muhammad's journey of ascendance to the heavens began from Jerusalem.

Palestine lies on the Mediterranean Sea across from Europe. It also separates the lands of Asia and Africa; more specifically, it separates the Arab countries in two bulks, one in Asia and the other in Africa. Palestine was a piece of land all invaders of different times found vital to control, for it is the main passage to the Middle East and North Africa.

Through my upbringing, I desperately wanted to know more about my background, my country, and my people. Questions like, who are the Palestinian people, arose in my mind. I started reading books about history, where I discovered how various historians traced the origins of the Palestinians. Most of them came close but, never found a definition which was accurate for the modern-day Palestinians. Are they Jebusites? Amorites? Arameans? Canaanites? Philistines? Hebrews? Arabs? Are they a historic mixture of all those people? All of them except the Philistines came from the same contiguous land, the Eastern Mediterranean. The Philistines, however, are traced by most historians to the Aegean Sea islands, Crete, and/or other nearby islands. Why did the Philistines settle in the land of Canaan? This was not well documented or well known, which led historians to develop a theory which concluded that the Philistines left their islands due to some natural catastrophe, such as volcanoes or severe earthquakes. The Philistines invaded the land of Canaan. After that, they fought many wars with Israelites and the old Egyptians. Eventually, the Philistines melded with the people of the area, mainly the Canaanites. It would be fair to say today that the Palestinians are a fair mixture, over centuries, made of the Canaanites as the biggest portion, and the Philistines, and the Arabs.

The Arab, Christian, and Islamic factors shaped most of the Palestinian modern history. For centuries, the presence of Judaism was symbolic, at best. Up until the turn of the twentieth century, Jews were a very small minority in historical Palestine; too small in numbers to pose any threat of change to the demographics of the land at the time. Jewish kingdoms ruled for about 250 years in Palestine; however, even according to religious history, Jewish tribes immigrated to the land of Canaan. Jewish kingdoms were established, ruled parts of Palestine, but not all of it. Then they were destroyed. Nonetheless, the original inhabitants remained. A good portion of Jews stayed and converted to Islam or Christianity and meshed within the Palestinian "melting pot." The presence of Arabs from the Arabian Peninsula was especially enhanced after the emergence of Islam.

History tells of many invasions by foreign armies, including the Assyrians, Egyptians, the Israelites, the Greeks led by Alexander the Great, and Romans. More recent were the many Crusades from Europe. The Crusaders created a cause . . . It was to rule Palestine and secure freedom of travel and movement of Christian pilgrims to the Holy Land from all over the world. Wars were fought frequently and for many decades at a time. The Crusaders were led by kings from many countries of Europe, England, Spain, France, and others. In the end, the Arabs, being the people of the land and the surrounding countries, united under Saladin, and liberated Jerusalem and all of Palestine. The European Crusaders were sent on ships back to Europe.

Thereafter, Palestine lived generally in peace for centuries. Muslims, Christians, and a small community of Jews coexisted in harmony. Rulers changed, depending on politics of the Islamic Empire.

Palestine and Lebanon are also smaller in size as compared to modern-day Syria. Its largest city, Damascus, was the first capital of a unified Muslim state. Founded by the Umayyad leader Abd al-

Malik ibn-Marwan, he was the first Umayyad caliph, the title of the sultan at the time. He was the first to unify the Muslim countries under one centralized government, after being divided under different rulers. Damascus continued to have major political and economic influence, especially on Palestine and Lebanon.

People traveled between the borders of what is today Syria, Lebanon, and Palestine frequently. Many resided in and moved back and forth between these countries. To this date, many families trace back their ancestry in all three countries. This setup continued to the point where all three countries were called "Bilad al-Sham," (Greater Syria). Lebanon and Palestine did not have their own centralized rulers. They were open territories with city rulers in Jerusalem, Acre, Tyre, and so on. Each ruler governed the city and the area surrounding it. Palestine did not have its own country ruler, king, or sultan.

The last phase of rule in Palestine was part of the Ottoman Empire. The capital was Istanbul. Governors of countries, regions, and cities within the empire were appointed by the sultan. The Ottomans ruled the Arab countries for over 400 years; their economic and cultural influence was very apparent. Even to this day, numerous similarities exist between Turkish and Arab culture.

Economies of Arab countries were subeconomies of the empire. Many laws and policies put upon those countries hindered the growth of most sectors of their local industries.

Prior to World War I, Western countries referred to the Ottoman Empire as "The Sick Man." Based on hegemonic appetite, power, and influence, the rising Western countries agreed to divide and share the Ottoman Empire amongst each other. A secret agreement known as Sykes-Picot, named after the two French and British diplomats who negotiated it, enforced an already existing occupation, like that of Algeria which was invaded by France in 1830, and Tunisia which France also occupied in the year 1880, then added more countries. Lebanon and Syria went to France's control; England got Egypt, Jordan, Iraq, the Arabian Peninsula, and Palestine, and Italy got Libya. The outcome of World War I was long-term mandates to rule for over 25 years, and many cases were much longer with different colonial occupations. For example, France invaded Algeria and annexed it. "Algeria is France" was a famous slogan used by French politicians and media. Algeria was under French occupation for 132 years before it was able to achieve its independence.

During the late era of the Ottoman Empire, Palestine was a thriving country with an educated elite, prosperous businesses, trade, agriculture, and tourism, as well as bustling cities and a countryside famous for its fields dotting the landscape.

Most Muslims feel a deep religious connection to Jerusalem. They aspire to visit and pray in Al-Aqsa Mosque. Such a trip is considered to complement their hajj, i.e., pilgrimage to Mecca. Jerusalem was the first *Qibla*, the holy place Muslims directed their prayers for more than a year and half while Mecca was still controlled by the pagans. Muslims from all over the world came to Jerusalem. Christian pilgrims also came to Jerusalem for centuries, and continue doing so to this day.

When I walked the streets of the Old City, I noticed its overwhelming character is primarily Muslim and Christian. Historical structures and holy places are prominent. Many Jewish worshipers consider Jerusalem the holiest of the holy places. They believe Solomon's Temple existed on the same hilltop where the Al-Aqsa Mosque stands today. This belief continues to create turmoil and conflict between Muslims and Jews. During one of my visits to Jerusalem, I saw small models of the city sold in Jewish antiquity stores. Ironically, the Muslim shrine did not exist in those models. It was replaced by the Jewish temple.

Al-Nakba

The word *Nakba*, ("catastrophe") defines the greatest historic event to have happened to the people of Palestine. In 1948, Israel was born and declared as a state. It was then that an undeclared death certificate of Palestine was issued. Suddenly, the people of Palestine were told their country, known to the rest of the world as Palestine, no longer existed, and they themselves were not a people. They just happened to live there. Israel was back from the dead, and Palestine was now dead.

The implications of the event shaped, and continue to shape, lives of Palestinians everywhere; it can never be forgotten. What happened to the Palestinian people cannot be compared to any other event in recent history. Not only a whole population of a country was terrorized, horrified, massacred, and chased out of their homes on a massive scale—they were also never allowed to return . . . while their country name was erased from geography books and renamed to become a homeland of another people.

Deir Yassin, a small Palestinian village on the outskirts of Jerusalem, was attacked by Irgun fighters. Irgun was one of the Jewish militant organizations which played a vicious role in the 1948 ethnic cleansing of Palestine. On April 9, 1948, innocent people, including women, children, and the elderly, were shot and killed. The whole village was inhabited by few hundred people, and at least 115 of them were killed.

The news of what happened in Deir Yassin traveled throughout Palestine. Stories of women raped were the straw that broke the camel's back. A Palestinian will fight and die for his land; however, the possibility of women getting raped pushed many to flee with their families.

Trucks and cars filled with explosives were sent by Jewish militants into Palestinian markets and set off. Each killed scores of people. Many people fled out of fear, after such events, or just before their cities and towns were surrounded by Jewish militants and attacked.

Zionist militants were equipped with far superior weaponry, including tanks, armored vehicles, artillery, and fighter planes. In addition to the underground Jewish army, the Haganah, Zionist forces included the Jewish army brigades which fought during WW II in Europe among the Allies. They were led by experienced generals who had fought many fierce battles. Facing them were

Palestinian peasants and city neighborhood youths, carrying light machine guns and pistols. Small battalions of the newly formed Syrian and Egyptian armies joined the war. However, they were no match for the Zionist forces and were doomed to defeat.

Palestinians, including my family, found themselves defenseless and helpless. People rushed about in fear and hastily grabbed anything which might help them on their trip. They thought they would be back after a few days or perhaps weeks, until the war settled, and then life would resume as it used to be. However, for most of them, it proved to be a one-way life-changing trip for generations afterwards. People exited their cities, towns, and villages, headed in all directions. Some went to the north, into Lebanon, or northeast into Syria. Others went to the east of Palestine, where some remained in what is known as the West Bank. Many continued into the country of Jordan. Scores of Palestinians also went south into the seaside strip of Gaza, which was protected by the presence of Egyptian troops. Others continued into Egypt.

The country was in chaos. Bodies lay in the streets. Homes were abandoned with open or unlocked doors. Men, women, pregnant women, children, and the elderly people rode cars, buses, boats, or even carriages pulled by horses and donkeys. Those who could not get access to some means of transportation just walked and walked for days. Many of the elderly, infants, and young children did not make it to those destinations. They died of sickness in the open fields.

In the book *The Birth of Israel*, authored by Israeli Professor Simha Flapan, he states how David Ben-Gurion was pleasantly astonished when he saw a whole city like Haifa in the north coastal part of Palestine emptied of its people. Jewish immigrants, could, and, in fact, did, move into already-existing homes. The original inhabitants of those homes were out in the wilderness, or in pitched tents, in massive numbers. Only some, who carried with them enough money, were able to rent homes to shelter their displaced families.

They all just waited every single day to hear on the radio that they could return to their homes and be safe. However, days became weeks, weeks became months, months became years, and years turned in to decades. The news never arrived.

 The cause of Palestine was born out of that great human tragedy. With passion and dedication, it was passed on from one generation of Palestinians to the next. To this day, the story of Nakba continues to be told by the elder to the younger Palestinian.

Like most children of Palestine at the time, I felt a great responsibility to reclaim our right to Palestine . . . to be able to go back to the homeland and take back what belonged to our aging parents and reinstate justice. Achieving that goal was considered a lifetime mission, to which every patriotic Palestinian felt an obligation to contribute. Nakba was a massive crime the whole world continued to deal with.

Diaspora

The people of Palestine were no longer in one country, identified by geography and history. They became scattered in what is left of Palestine and the surrounding Arab countries. From there, another wave of immigration began to different countries of the world. The need for survival made any place in the world desirable as long as it offered work. Palestinians started losing their recognized unity as a people of a country and a national identity. They were referred to as "Palestinian refugees." Over time, the world communities dropped their belonging to their country, and addressed their problem as a problem of refugees needing to resettle somewhere—anywhere—and to just dissolve and disappear as a people. Many Arab countries were encouraged to offer them citizenship, but only a few became citizens in the countries where they resided.

Palestinians maintained their status of refugees. Most countries offered refugee identity cards, and later temporary travel documents, special made and issued. In countries like Lebanon, Palestinians were not allowed to work. Later, a few job types were allowed . . . only those which required hard labor. Unfortunately, these laws are still in place to this day. Lebanese laws specifically forbid Palestinians to own homes. Those who owned one prior to the law taking affect can't pass such property to their heirs. A home owned by a Palestinian in Lebanon must be sold to a non-Palestinian when he or she dies. To be fair, a great many Lebanese feel ashamed of such a law. Other countries like Syria, Jordan, and Egypt were more relaxed about allowing Palestinians to work and own businesses. The Palestinians were known to be honest, hardworking, educated, and dedicated to improve their lives.

Palestine was so close geographically, yet, at times, seemed like it was so far away. Its former citizens were burdened by so many obstacles, including the needs surrounding everyday living. I observed how many Lebanese were resentful of the Palestinian presence in their country. Many Lebanese treated us as a burden, and sadly, in some ways, we were. Lebanon is a small country with very limited resources. They did not have enough economic opportunities for their own citizens. However, I could not understand the everyday ill treatment that we were subjected to for just being Palestinians. In addition to the lack of freedom of movement, a lack of civil rights, and absence of hope, we experienced daily mockery and mortification.

Fathers and young men tried very hard to travel to other countries. They yearned to better themselves and their situation. An economic boom started in the oil-rich Arab countries. Some Palestinians traveled to those countries with no visa. They crossed several countries illegally to enter a country like Kuwait. Some of them died in the desert before getting there. They paid human smugglers to get them to their destination. It was their ambition to reach there. Once they arrived, they put their pride aside and accepted any job they could get. They accepted the consequences of living there without any security, possibly getting arrested, and even thrown in jail for entering the country illegally. Or, they could simply be deported back to where they came from. But they were thankful to be there, and that they had a chance to earn a living. They were grateful for anything that kept them from getting sent back to their refugee camps, where the conditions were wretched, they were helpless, and unemployed. They were desperate.

Some of them made a decent income and were able to save money, which helped them climb out of the hole they were forced into. Others somehow managed to travel beyond the oceans. To their families and loved ones, they became like a shadow in the faraway distance. They hoped their loved ones would come back someday. Many left as young men, only to return much older.

That was the beginning of the Palestinian Diaspora. Many Palestinians lost the daily presence of their nuclear family at an early age. Most young men, married or not, had to leave for another country, wherever work was offered. They came from the refugee camps of Lebanon, Jordan, Iraq, Syria, and Egypt, the West Bank, and Gaza.

The Old City of Acre (Akka), a view from the south

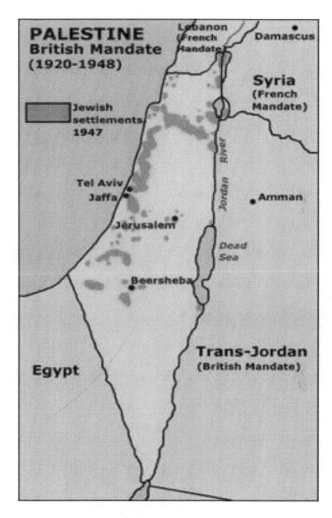

Map of Palestine in 1947

1948 Ethnic Cleansing of Palestine, Nakba

The Right of Return key, a symbol passed from one generation to the next

Chapter 2

Sabra, Born and Raised

I did not live in a refugee camp. My family was lucky enough to have had some means to allow us to avoid tents, where most of the Palestinians who fled Palestine ended up. As years went by, those tents changed to structures covered by zinc panels, and supported by wood on the inside. With time, they became dwellings, with no bathrooms or running water; no heating in the cold winters. Many of them were overrun and flooded by severe rainstorms. Families grouped in minicompounds. The refugee dwellings were almost attached to one another. Inside them were families who slept on homemade mattresses or poor quality sponge mattresses provided by the United Nations aid organizations. A camp with several thousand people had one small area where primitive restrooms were built, and one container from which people filled their buckets with drinking water every morning.

Likewise, people formed long lines to use filthy and unsanitary public restrooms. There were public baths in the adjacent neighborhood, where people went to bathe every few days. Little canals of dirty wastewater ran between the houses as the water flowed to the edge of the camps. For health care, there was a small clinic with a very limited medical capacity; one doctor and a locally trained nurse dealt with too many people's medical needs. Regardless of the disease or illness, people were prescribed the same medicines due to the shortage of supplies. Dawa Ahmar, a red liquid, some kind of bacterial cleaner, was commonly prescribed, to the point that Palestinians made many jokes regarding it and sang satirical songs about it. Periodically, people in the camp gathered at the United Nations aid center to collect their monthly allotment of flour and rice, and sometimes other donations were given to help them survive.

I was born in Sabra, a poor suburb of Beirut, a place where low to extremely very low-income Palestinian refugees and Lebanese lived, and still do. The two communities mixed and matched in many ways. Many times, they came together united for a certain purpose, mostly political or religious. I felt the differences and tension during our day-to-day life, either when the Palestinians felt they were being mistreated (which was the norm), or when the Lebanese felt Palestinians were gaining too much power (which rarely occurred). Politically, however, most of the time, these two communities agreed, which showed, underneath, they did have a lot in common. They supported the same local leaders, allied with the same regional Pan-Arab leaders, rallied together in the same demonstrations, and fought together a civil unrest in the 1950s, which was, at the time, supported by the late Nasser, the well-known Pan-Arab leader.

I often sat on the little balcony outside the kitchen of our small two-bedroom apartment, the place where my family lived. I stared at the mountains, mostly at night. I was mesmerized by the lights of the homes in the distance, a sight which felt peaceful and detached from the noisy neighborhood where I lived. I imagined and admired the kind of life the people where those tiny lights shone in the far distance must be experiencing. Those thoughts made me feel a part of this big world, so that I was not confined by the limited dreams Sabra had to offer.

My family consisted of three sisters, three brothers, my mother and father, grandfather, grandmother, two uncles, two aunts—all from my father's side—living in the same home. I was the fifth one born. Actually, I was number six, since my firstborn brother died in a very sad accident. He fell off the patio of my parents' home in Palestine. He was less than a year old. His name was Mahmoud, the same as my grandfather's name. The custom was the oldest son is named after his grandfather. His memory remained alive. He was mentioned every now and then as a very beautiful and smart child. The accident never left my mother's memory.

I also had an uncle I never met. His name was Rafik, and he lived and died in Palestine. Mahmoud and my uncle were both buried in Acre Cemetery. Their tombs were next to those of great-grandfathers and -grandmothers. Rafik, like the rest of Palestinians who did not flee, never reunited with his family and relatives. He was married to a Jewish/Israeli lady with a Ukrainian background and had six children with her. He was known to be superhandsome and a very proud man. He also loved to live well and had a hot temper. He could never accept his new reality, that all his brothers, sisters, mother and father left Acre and did not, nor could they, return. Inside, he was a very sad person.

When I was about 9 years old, Uncle Rafik rented a speedboat and rode it all the way to Sidon, crossing the marine borders between Israel and Lebanon. I still can't decide if that was brave or pure crazy. Had he been discovered by an Israeli naval force, his boat could have been hit by a torpedo rocket. An unidentified boat presence was suspected as enemy activity. He crossed the heavily secured and monitored border area into Lebanese waters, and into the port of the southern city of Sidon. He anchored his boat, and went straight to a police station. When he explained where he came from, and that he was in Lebanon to meet his relatives, the police detained him, but somehow they managed to contact our family. Only one of his brothers was allowed to see him before he was handed over, along with the boat, to the Red Cross, which, in turn, handed him over to Israeli authorities. He spent a couple of months in jail, and then was set free. My only explanation of the incident was that my uncle Rafik was a man torn between the past and the present. He used to send very sad letters which were carried to Beirut with an elderly man or a woman, who was allowed to visit Acre for a month via the Red Cross (as was allowed on a few occasions by Israeli authorities).

My uncle had many fights with my father's former partner in Acre, who managed to take over my father's share of the business. My uncle could not bear to see my father's ownership of his assets disappear and just stand by helpless and not be able to stop it. He also witnessed his father's house and other family properties get confiscated by Israeli authorities. The properties were labeled as "Properties of the absentee." Eventually, a special authority was formed by Israel's government, which took ownership of all Palestinian properties. They then sold some, leased others, and demolished what was deemed unsafe to keep. All refugees in Lebanon—like my parents—and elsewhere lost their ownership by confiscation based on an Israeli law, which penalized them for not paying property taxes—despite the fact that it was impossible for them to do so since they were not allowed back into their country.

Rafik lived the rest of his life troubled and unhappy. When he was 50 while walking a street in the city of Haifa, an object fell from a building, hit him on the head, and caused him serious head injury, which eventually paralyzed him from the waist down. He attempted suicide twice . . . The second time he was successful. He ended his own life at the age of 52, feeling helpless to support his family and having given up on life.

During my childhood, our small home was filled with people. Three different families lived in the two-bedroom, one-bath apartment. Half of our living room was converted to a bedroom. Many mattresses were stored on top of each other in a storage area, unfolded in the evening and spread throughout the place, so we could all sleep. The overcrowded apartment held tension, criticism, arguing, and fighting. This went on for a few years, until such time that my aunt's family was able to rent their own place. My single aunt Anisa and my two uncles traveled to an Arab gulf country for work. After that, the atmosphere in our home became better for me growing up than it had been for my older brothers and sisters.

At the age of 4, I was sent daily to a kindergarten in the heart of Sabra. However, somehow, the place was different in culture from its surroundings. It was a nice happy place. I played and learned new things; the teachers were very nice women. That was where, for the first time, I learned of and actually saw a Santa Clause or "Papa Noel," as he is commonly known in Lebanon. I even received gifts. I used to walk to that kindergarten from home and back. I once saw Samih, my older brother, on the street close by. I shouted his name. I was sure my brother heard and saw me, but for some reason, he ignored me and left. I was a little hurt and confused, but later found out that he was ditching school that day. He did not want me to tell on him. Samih hated going to school and got into a lot of trouble with our father because of that.

I learned of death in my early years of kindergarten. I was going back home from kindergarten and my grandfather died that day. The family just sent me to kindergarten and did not tell me anything about it. No one explained to me what it was all about. I was sad, and I did not know how to understand my feelings when someone is gone forever. It was difficult for me, as a child, to comprehend that I would never see that person again. In his old age, my grandfather sometimes dressed up in the Qumbaz, a traditional Syrian Arab man's clothing, and put on a Tarboush, a red cylindrical-shaped Turkish hat, a common look for men of his generation. During his last few years, he sometimes thought he was still in Acre and wanted to go to the souk, the market, and meet his friends. I strongly felt his sudden disappearance. His small converted bedroom became empty, his little bed and few belongings were gone. I remember how I used to greet him, and how he greeted me back. He was a loving person. I just stored his memory in my mind and moved on.

My memories of all my family members being together were scarce and only consisted of a short period of time, maybe 3 years. It felt very short. By the time I was 6, my eldest sister Suhair was married and moved with her husband to Saudi Arabia where her husband worked. Shortly after that, my oldest brother Walid left for Tripoli, a city in the north of Lebanon for his high school. From there, he traveled to Egypt for his university studies. A year after, my sister Samira traveled to Kuwait for work; a year later, my brother Samih was sent off to a technical school where he learned to be a machinist and an electric welder. Then he traveled to Libya, where he got a job. Walid had to discontinue his pursuit of an engineering degree and went to work in Saudi Arabia because our family finances were low and needed support. We could not afford to wait for him to graduate. Our aunt Anisa, the sweetest and most caring person I ever met, worked as a tailor for a modest income to help our family. She spent the years of her youth doing that. She never had the chance to get married and have a family of her own.

Being the youngest son, I watched my brothers and sisters go away, one after the other. Our household was down to just me and my younger sister Salma. We were still in elementary school. During that time in my life, I did not have a close relationship with my father. I remember my father going to work and coming back home. Frequently, he bought fruit along the way. My mother was closer to me. Her character left a huge impact on me. She appeared to me as a very strong woman, very caring, but also very tough and harsh at times. During traditional celebrations of the Muslim holidays, when kids would wear new clothes, she took me shopping for new clothes as well, and made sure my younger sister and I had nice clothes to wear.

I realized early on in my life that my father and mother had a traditionally arranged marriage, which was very common for their generation. They did not have a chance to meet and get to know each other before they wed. I got to know my father much better at an older age. Despite his emotional distance during my childhood, he cared to make sure my character was proud and dignified. One time, I unexpectedly visited him at his tailor shop in Beirut. He received me well and bought me some goodies from the grocer across the street. I felt I wanted to help, so I picked up a broom and tried to sweep the floor of his shop, but my dad gently told me to quit and made me understand this kind of work was not for me. He wanted me to be a respected visitor. Although only a small act, it boosted my self-respect and confidence. I then sat back and behaved like a dignified visitor.

My father knew my school principal. Occasionally he would ask him how I was doing, and we would have a discussion if there was a complaint. He also showed me how he was very proud of me when I was among the top three students in my class. His recognition made me want to stay at that level. After that, I could not stand the thought of not being at the top of my class, or at least the second-best student. My father, since my early childhood, constantly stressed that I had to become better, stronger, and certainly, more educated. "Palestine was lost because of a lack of education of its people," he said. Our people, generally, could not analyze what was going on around them at the time and did not know how to react to the events or how to plan to defend their homeland.

My first grade was at a "mixed" school, where both boys and girls attended. I remember my first day, I had a knot in my stomach because I was so stressed out, and I was very shy and found it difficult to talk to anyone. Soon after, I earned the admiration of my teacher for being such a good student. I still felt I would be more comfortable in an all-boys nearby school, so I finally was able to join it the year after. That was the place where not only was I getting education, but also, it was where I started understanding what it meant to be Palestinian.

Jaffa Elementary School, named after the ancient Palestinian seaport city Jaffa, was not an ordinary elementary school. It was a reflection of the refugees' lives, hardships, desperation, deprivation, and memories of Palestine. However, most important was how it planted hopeful dreams of the future. Teachers played a great role in making me understand the different pieces of the political puzzle. They taught and explained what Palestinian national interests were and what were not. To them, teaching was not just a job, it was a national duty. The Palestinians understood that ignorance was as dangerous an enemy as the one that drove them out of their country. It was shameful to fall behind in school. Most students put a lot of effort into their work. We wanted to prove that we were worthy, if not excellent.

Sabra the old neighborhood

Chapter 3

Nasser of Egypt

I was little over 10 years old, and by then, it was 19 years since the Nakba. The Palestinians had many hopes in the famous Pan-Arabist leader of Egypt, Gamal Abdel Nasser. After all, he was the president of the largest, most populous Arab country, which was the birthplace of many aspects of human civilization. As an army officer, Nasser fought in Palestine against the Zionist army and organizations in 1948. He went back to Egypt with a defeat which scarred his national dignity. Egypt was ruled by a very corrupt monarchy, including a class of royals and pashas, a noble title granted by the king, men who were feudal lords, who owned the land and dictated the lives of its people.

Nasser organized a group of army officers like himself. Most of them were not top officers of the Egyptian army but rather midlevel officers. They needed a high-ranking figure and found one in army General Mohamed Naguib. Together, they carried out a coup d'état against the king and declared a revolution against the monarchy. They changed Egypt's political regime from a monarchy to a republic. Mohamed Naguib was appointed as the first president of the republic. In reality, Nasser and his comrade officers' group known as "The Free Army Officers," were the leaders and the decision makers. To Naguib's disappointment, he could not gain enough popularity to enable him to take control. Shortly after, Naguib gave the Free Officers an ultimatum with a demand to surrender most controlling powers to him. The Free Officers declined, he resigned, and a new star was on the rise. His name, Gamal Abdel Nasser.

By Arab standards, Nasser was tall, dark, and handsome with a great charisma. He was a magnetic speaker. I remember at the age of 10, when Gamal Abdel Nasser was delivering a speech, I used to see people on the streets in small crowds, each crowd surrounding a loud radio. No one talked. Everything in the neighborhood was quiet and came to a standstill . . . except for the loud voice of the man loved and admired by millions of Arabs. When that was going on in Beirut, it was also happening in all of Lebanon, of course in Egypt, and almost all the Arab countries. Even people in countries with regimes which opposed Nasser heard his speeches quietly and privately in their own homes. The day Nasser spoke, most Arabs listened . . . in a big way. He indeed unified most of the Arab people, at least in our hearts. He believed in Arab unity, social justice, and democracy, and strongly promoted his cause. He was considered a threat to many regimes which did not share his ideas.

Nasser declared nationalization of the Suez Canal, which made it wholly owned by Egypt after decades of French and British hegemony. His decision led to a war with France, England, and particularly Israel, which found in that crisis a great opportunity to defeat a growing power on its southern borders threatening its existence. Especially since Nasser supported the Palestinians and their right to their homeland. That war became known as the 1956 Suez Canal War. Egypt was attacked and had no chance against its three enemies. However, it was the United States of

America which interfered. The U.S. issued an ultimatum, which led to a cease-fire and withdrawal of the invading armies. Judging by the end result, the war was viewed by most of the Arab nation as a big victory for Egypt and its leader, Gamal Abdel Nasser. Even more important, a victory for the Arab people.

Popular resistance organized by Nasser's regime fought street battles in Port Said and Suez. A great many volunteers, such as Palestinians, Lebanese, Syrians, and many other Arab countries joined the Egyptian resistance. A song became famous in the Arab countries expressing support for Nasser. "From the rumbling ocean to the gulf of revolution (two borders of Arab countries), Nasser, we will heed your call."

Nasser inspired a generation of the Arab people. He also implemented historic reforms in Egypt. He redistributed the agricultural lands to the poor peasants and made them owners of the land they worked. He gave them back their pride and dignity.

Nasser's era created major growth of the industrial sector of Egypt. Large-scale steel, cement, even car assembly plants were created. In addition, he built the great Aswan Dam, which, for the first time in the history of Egypt, controlled the flow of the Nile River and distributed its water to better benefit agriculture. It also prevented the river from rising and flooding, which, in the past, caused many disasters for the people and the land.

Millions of Arabs believed Nasser was the man to unify Arab countries as one nation and lead the liberation of Palestine. Many believed at the time that if Nasser was to run for president in any Arab country, he would have won. Nasser had the support of individuals, and many parties in most Arab countries.

That era was the height of Arab unity aspirations. Egypt and Syria declared both their countries as one republic, with Nasser as the president. Arab people were exuberant with the hope unity would spread to all Arab countries. Unfortunately, it did not. It was an ill-fated union which was short-lived. It ended up with a separation of the two regimes, and with that, it left the Arab people suffering a great disappointment.

The 1967 War

A few years later, tensions with Israel heightened due to Nasser's accumulated successes at home, both economically and militarily . . . and more importantly was his growing sphere of influence. A new crisis with Israel came to surface in 1967. It was aggravated by a dispute over the presence of a United Nations peacekeeping force, which separated the Egyptian and the Israeli armies. The UN force withdrawal was followed by a full war. Israel carried out a large-scale, all-out attack on Egypt. The next 6 days witnessed a slaughter of a large number of Egyptian soldiers. The Israeli air force attacked and destroyed the entire Egyptian air force while most Egyptian warplanes were on the ground at their bases. Egyptian ground soldiers were left on the front lines with no air cover. They became like sitting ducks to the Israeli fighter planes and bombers, which decimated thousands and fragmented the remainder. A similar scenario was taking place on the Syrian-Israeli front, and the Jordanian-Israeli front.

An Arab national disaster happened in 6 days of war. Many events took place as a result of the defeat. Arab people in all countries blamed their leaders and regimes. People of Egypt and Syria, for the first time since the creation of Israel, lost part of their land to the Israeli occupation. Egypt lost Gaza and the entire Sinai Desert. The IDF was stationed on the opposite bank of the Suez Canal. Syria lost the Golan Heights, a beautiful, fertile mountainous landscape with water and a strategic military location overlooking historical Palestine. Jordan lost control of the West Bank of the Jordan River, which was annexed to the kingdom of Jordan upon a truce agreement with Israel in 1948. We were devastated by that defeat. Palestine was pushed farther away from us. Hopes of Nasser liberating Palestine were replaced by a horrible route of Arab armies.

The Arab people's blood was boiling with anger. They wanted accountability for this failure. Those regimes which bragged about their power and readiness to fight Israel, that had predicted victory, were shaken with shame and humiliation. The Egyptian army became the butt of jokes by its people.

Nasser spoke to his people and the whole Arab nation, announced his resignation, and took full responsibility; however, the people trusted and loved him and did not want to see him go. Egyptians came out in millions right after he finished his speech. They crowded the streets of Cairo, filled the streets for miles between Nasser's home and the parliament, and demanded he stay on as their leader, chanting: "We will fight! We will fight!" "Nasser!" "Nasser!" None of that was staged or preplanned. It was emotionally moving to watch on television. I was not quite yet 12 years old, but that did not prevent me from going out in the streets and joining hundreds of thousands in a massive show of love and trust in an Arab leader we regarded with the highest levels of admiration. Nasser inspired and moved us, no matter how difficult victory was to achieve. He represented

Arab national dignity under all circumstances. The street scene was overwhelming in magnificence. Nasser, who was genuine about leaving politics, was moved to his core by that historic event. It was a voice which could not be ignored. The event went on and on until Nasser withdrew his resignation. He was back with full confidence.

Nasser later revamped his regime. Many strong figures fell from favor and were held accountable. Most influential was Abdel Hakim Amer, the army commander and Nasser's comrade in struggle, who played a vital role in the Egyptian revolution.. He was subjected to questioning about his miserable performance and misleading Nasser and Egypt about the true state of the army. Hakim's monopoly of power over the Egyptian army during his tenure did not help either. It made him much more accountable. To avoid what seemed to be a predictable fate, he then planned and tried to execute a coup attempt to topple Nasser. However, his plan was aborted by an early intervention of Nasser's supporters. Hakim was put under house arrest. He was later found shot dead in his house. It was declared a suicide. Whether he committed suicide or was assassinated remains a mystery.

Nasser went on to rebuild his army and pressured the Soviet Union to provide the Egyptians with an effective air defense system and more advanced weapons. The Soviets promised and delivered.

Meanwhile, in Syria, a successful military coup was carried out by Hafez al-Assad, defense minister at the time, and Baath Party leader. He toppled the presidency of Attasi. Assad blamed Attasi for the 1967 war defeat and imprisoned him. Then Assad became the president instead.

Assad took control of Syria and continued to be a feared leader until his death in the year 2000. Security forces, including secret police, intruded into the everyday lives of Syrians, violated civil rights, and the freedom of expression. It was a totalitarian party system, despite allowing the presence of other small parties. Assad also rebuilt the Syrian army with help from the Soviets. And later, it showed it was able to perform well.

Nasser (4th from the right), Nagib (2nd from right), Hakim (3rd from the right) and other leaders of the Egypt revolution

Nasser, Popular leader of Egypt and Arab masses

Chapter 4

Liberation Movement

At the age of 12, I heard the news of Palestinians taking matters in their own hands. The word reached Palestinian refugees in Lebanon. It also reached the Palestinians everywhere in the world. Palestinian politics were still handled by a defeated generation, despite a segment of the young who wanted to fight back. Some joined groups which fought along the borders and in the Gaza Strip. Those groups were small and fragmented.

University students everywhere debated about what was to be done. Among them was a man named Yasser Arafat, who lived in Egypt during that time. Arafat and a few of his close comrades founded "Fatah." It emerged as a Palestinian-born group independent of any Arab regime. It was defiant and carried the Palestinian pain and pride. Unlike previously created organizations, Fatah claimed to be dependent only on the people and promised not to be a disappointment. Fatah did not wait for Egypt or Syria or any other country to lead the battle of liberation. The new movement brought about support beyond anyone's imagination. Only a few confrontations with Israel were sufficient. Guerilla war-style battles were enough to give Fatah the credibility needed. Hundreds of thousands rallied behind it. It became the hope and the future, and it represented the Palestinian national aspirations.

Stories about a group called Fidayeen, life-sacrificing fighters for liberation, inspired people. Palestinians imagined the Fidayeen as superheroes, well trained, strong, and brave, fighting and standing up to the Israeli soldiers. They mounted successful attacks which embarrassed the Israeli army and shattered their reputation of being undefeatable. Palestinian men, young and old, and many women wanted to join them to bring back the pride of the past to the present.

The Palestinians by then were sick and tired of their humiliating life without many rights granted to them. They wanted to return to their homeland. Those in the refugee camps had had enough empty promises and false hopes publicized throughout the

Arab media. Palestine, from the beginning of its tragedy, was glorified in the media. However, the reality is that the Palestinian refugees were—and still are—poorly treated by most Arab governments. Generally, a few of these governments granted them some rights to allow them the bare essentials of life in the countries where they found themselves despite being there against their will. And even those countries treated them with a great degree of disrespect and kept them feeling vulnerable and insecure. The Palestinians looked everywhere in the world for that respect and those common basic rights which would allow them to make a decent life, a life where one could work hard, earn a living, and help the families they left behind in the refugee camps.

Many powerful countries of the world believed that by improving the Palestinian living conditions, this would eventually dissolve their aspirations of going back to their homeland Palestine. But the problem was far greater than that. These very same countries failed to look at the Palestinians as a people. The word *Palestine* was meant to disappear from the face of the earth and just become dead history. When a Palestinian was asked, "Where are you from?" and he answered, "I am from Palestine," his answer was met with shock and astonishment, particularly in Western countries. Palestinians did not know what to say about their national identity. They were being forced to deny their national heritage while they only carried a temporary travel document which stated they were Palestinian refugees.

Palestinian modern national uprising started at the time when accumulation of events and hardship of life caused by Nakba created a catalyst, which ignited the struggle of a people. It was the start of a revolution to change the status quo. Even though it was undermined by many opposing powers, it grew against all odds. Many highly respected politicians on the world stage, and many intellectuals and thinkers discounted it as a cause with no means of continuity. Many thought the Palestinians will settle and disburse around the world, and Palestine will disappear forever; they never did, and neither did Palestine.

The Palestinians in the old homeland lived in much worse conditions, yet struggled to keep their national identity. Numbered under two hundred thousand were those who remained behind after cities and villages were left completely vacant, when newcomers from different areas of the world occupied these same houses and made them their own. A new state was born, and those Palestinians who stayed were not welcome. They were forced to confine themselves and move around only with security passes. It's like one would wake up one day and find himself in the same place but everything around him changed—different people, language, and culture. They survived all that; they were meant to remain frozen in time, live in the forties as the world around them moved on into the fifties, sixties, and beyond. This went on until the new state of Israel had to struggle with its own identity, as part of the West who take pride in democracy and freedom as its pillars, and yet, Israel, the new democracy of the time, oppressed the native people! Not exactly a good image, not for the new Israeli generations and certainly not to the modern world which had just defeated Nazism.

That had to change. It did, however, only minimally, not to cause a huge racist scene, but it fell short of full citizenship rights. Although they were made citizens of Israel, their citizenship status remained an issue of debate among some Jewish Israelis. By the year 2000, Palestinians in the state of Israel counted more than a million and a half, constituting 20 percent of the state's citizens, yet their level of representation and their growth ratio are far under that percentage. They still have to fight to earn their right to progress in life, and they are doing a great job at it. Today, many of them have become scientists, doctors, lawyers, engineers, professors, poets, authors, and other professionals as well as great community leaders who so eloquently define their struggle for survival against the continuous threat of "Transfer," the new civilized term for "ethnic cleansing."

Today, the new political cause in the Israeli politics is for Israel to be recognized by the Palestinians first, and then the rest of the world as a "Jewish state," a demand which seems to be so strange in today's world . . . and why would the Palestinians do that? Why would anyone agree to have no potential to grow and dream of major influence in his country? Must a Palestinian who is now an Israeli citizen never dream of becoming a president of the state since he is not Jewish? How does such a political regime reconcile with democracy? So far, not only are world democracies mostly silent about it, but also presidents of major Western democratic countries publicly support it. No one came out to say *this is not a model we want in a world where a black man became the president of the United States only after two generations when blacks were not allowed to mix with whites even on a bus.*

Somehow, the Western world behaved as though the Palestinians just hated the West, in general, and hated the United States, in particular, in addition to hating Israel . . . even hating the Jews for being Jews, a perception which spread throughout the Western world. I felt resentment at what looked like an absolute unquestionable and unconditional support for Israel, whether right or wrong—and almost always at the expense of Palestinian rights. It seemed at the time no matter which Western media source I listened to or watched, it was anti-Palestinian. Some Palestinians unintentionally contributed to this perception through desperate acts, even though their violent acts were intended to promote the cause. Acts similar to the Munich kidnapping of Israeli athletes, during the Olympic events of 1972, which led to a shooting battle, rather than forcing their demands on Israel. Gunfights broke out between the Germans and the Palestinian kidnappers. As a result, most of the athletes and kidnappers were killed. The incident brought attention to the Palestinian cause, for sure, however, it was negative, and it served for many years to label the Palestinian struggle as one of terrorists who had no respect for human life.

Many Palestinian active groups were engaged in acts of revenge, rather than building up a case and show the justice of the Palestinian cause. Their acts were mixed and confused for many years, something which became hard to change, even to this day. Suicide bombers attacking civilian targets reinforced that wrong perception. If the Palestinians were clear from the beginning about a set of values and stuck to the nobility of their struggle, and took all the sacrifices they were required to make by not reacting with desperate acts of revenge, they would've been better off. However, they did not for the longest time, and when they finally did, the whole world could no longer ignore them. If an enemy is the aggressor and kills your innocent ones, you should not kill his innocent ones, no matter what, because this will place you morally in the same category, and show that you have the same set of beliefs as your enemy's. Therefore, you are not worthy of support, although you were the victim to begin with.

The Palestinians did not help their own cause when they took actions which shocked the world, and some of those acts resulted in the death of innocent people, particularly in the West. It started with the hijacking of civilian airplanes and culminated with the hostage taking of the Israeli athletes at the Olympics in Munich, Germany. These acts followed the Palestinians for many years after and were used against them in every possible forum.

Being part of all this was difficult, to say the least. Feelings of isolation and longing to belong are emotions the Palestinian carries with him wherever he is. Being stripped of a homeland deconstructs one's roots. The feeling passes on from one generation to another. It is possible only for a very small minority to decide to bury and mourn Palestine in their minds and try to blend in a different country which offers them citizenship.

Palestine started to be created in my mind and my imagination at a very early stage of life. I wanted to be part of the struggle, to contribute and to identify with it more with every passing day. When I was in my last year in elementary school, I decided, along with a few of my classmates, to join the new faction "Fatah" which became more popular every day and gained respect. It was considered a great honor to be part of that movement. Young Palestinians heard they could actually be members. One major problem, however . . . The group, at that time, did not have bases in Lebanon. There were only secret members. Fatah was fully active in Syria. We decided to go to them since they can't come to us.

But how would we get there? We were too young to travel and legally cross borders, so we naïvely decided to cross the mountains to the very east of Lebanon, which were the geographical borders between Lebanon and Syria.

One day five of us met, as planned, got on a bus which traveled east to the Bekaa Valley. We got off the bus, crossed the valley field toward the foothills of the eastern mountains. From there, we started our hiking trip to cross the border. I remember we had our books with us. I don't know why we were still carrying our books, but once we were up on the mountains, we became very thirsty. Our books were covered with nylon covers, which we used to wrap them with it to better protect them. We took off those nylon covers and grabbed some of the snow which sporadically dotted the hills, and wrapped it with the nylon sheet. Then we waited for the snow to melt so we could drink the water. We kept walking, and the day finally came to its end. Once the sun set, the weather changed. It rained on us. We were in a very remote, wild area and started seeing wild animals running in the distance . . .

foxes and coyotes. We became thirsty again. We were walking to no particular destination on the horizon, when we saw a little pond in the distance. We ran to it where we thought we could get some freshwater. As we approached it, I looked into the water and saw different kinds of insects. I screamed to everyone not to drink it, because I thought we could get gravely ill and possibly die. My friends agreed.

As it became darker, we felt cold and scared, and with no glimpse of civilized life anywhere, doubt and fear took over. Four of us started talking about going back, but our stubborn friend, Bahjat, strongly disagreed and wanted us to continue our adventure. When we stopped, he actually went on farther, but the rest of us turned back. We told him he could go by himself, if that was his desire, so we parted ways. But shortly afterward, he turned back and joined us.

Going back was a good feeling, the trip back was easier, and as we went down the hill to the nearest village, we looked for any shop where we could buy some food—any food, because by then we were starved. We found a little shop and bought some bread, Labneh, a popular milk by-product, and olives and we ate with voracious appetites. After that, we walked to find a bus heading back to Beirut. When we arrived, we learned our families discovered our plan and felt helpless, not knowing what to do, but despite being angry with us, they still received us with open arms and were very happy to see us.

The next day, I was home in bed, sick with a severe cold I caught on our trip, and I had a nosebleed so bad that I remember the scared faces of my family around my bed because the bleeding at the time wouldn't stop. When I recovered after a couple of days, I went back to school, and to my surprise, even though my teachers did not agree with what we did, my friends and I became well respected and everyone treated us like heroes, especially the students. We earned a leadership position in a way. I felt I had to live up to my newly earned status by also being a good example, and went on to study hard. I passed the elementary official tests, then moved on to middle school.

Some of our elementary and middle school teachers did not just teach us school academic material; they also refined our nationalism, along with the Palestinian older generation who passed on to us the recent history of losing our homeland. They explained the roles and responsibilities of the powers in the world around us. At a very young age we formed an understanding of who we were, and what happened to our parents. Not only that, they passed on the responsibility to us to regain our lost country and our lost pride. They made sure we understood that the lack of education was a big factor and we had to make up for it by becoming outstanding individuals. That belief was the major motivation for success a whole generation accomplished across the world, wherever the Palestinian generation of the Nakba went. For the most part, they became successful, in almost every field. Successful engineers, entrepreneurs, and scientists emerged from among young men who were raised in refugee camps. A couple of them even became scientists in the United States. Many contributed to the development of the Gulf Arab states in many sectors of the economy. The success story of this generation was never told as it deserves to be told to this day. It is a great story of life struggles, sacrifices, and success.

The new movement gained popularity among students and other communities. Fatah grew strong enough that it took over the existing Palestine Liberation Organization (PLO), an umbrella organization (semigovernment in exile) made of many parties, factions, and Palestinian society leaders known to be independent of party affiliations. Nasser supported the PLO. It was also recognized by most Arab governments as the political representative of the Palestinians. A new national council (semiparliament) was elected, which, in turn, elected Yasser Arafat as the new chairman of the PLO. It became a new and reformed PLO, one which was more representative of the Palestinian people and their will.

The PLO went on to consolidate its status by gaining recognition of the Arab League, where all the Arab countries were members. The PLO was admitted as a member and the representative of the Palestinians, something King Hussein of Jordan resisted, since the West Bank was annexed to his kingdom and its Palestinian inhabitants were made Jordanian citizens. In addition to that, hundreds of thousands of Palestinian refugees were already living in Jordan.

The emergence of the current Palestinian national movement was moving in full gear, while the rest of the world was simply trying to place Palestine in the section of what seemed as deleted countries and forgotten people.

Anything to do with Palestinians was merely an annoyance. Their problem was considered a refugee problem and was dealt with accordingly. On the maps, there was no such place as Palestine. It was claimed that Palestinians can trace back their origins in the surrounding Arab countries and should actually live in these countries and just assimilate in them. Well, this was far from happening, and the passing days and years proved it wrong; neither the Palestinians nor the Arab people wanted it. What happened to the Palestinians was a national catastrophe which can't be dissolved and buried, no matter how much some of the most influential powers of the world wanted it to.

Fatah also very much appealed to Arab people at large, and hundreds, if not thousands, of Arab young men traveled to Jordan and later to Lebanon to join the liberation struggle.

I was among those who joined in their early teens. The doctrine Fatah adopted was very open-minded and inclusive. It kept a distance from limiting ideologies, whether religious, communist, socialist, or even Pan-Arab.

Somehow, the founders were very successful in creating a common denominator to all of them; it was sympathetic to all these ideologies and beliefs; however, it stopped short of fully adopting any of them. Everyone found a home in Fatah. That was its genius. It managed to convince the majority of active Palestinians that it was a liberation movement, which is Palestinian-driven at heart, and that it was still ideologically evolving. Its pillars were secular. The ultimate goal was to create a Palestinian democratic state where Palestinians and

Jews will have equal rights in one state. That was the popular magic which attracted all those with different ideological and political backgrounds.

As Fatah grew larger than its own founders imagined, it, as a political body, needed more money and political recognition. It's policy of nonintervention in internal Arab affairs (a slogan interpreted rightfully by Arab regimes and governments as "coexistence"), rather than being antagonistic and supportive of local opposition parties, made Fatah leaders welcome in those Arab capitals, and later made it possible to raise needed funds and seek recognition. It also strengthened the PLO status within the Arab states league. The PLO was able to gain support in both money and legitimacy, and moved on to the international political arena. It then started getting recognition in the United Nations, where eventually Yasser Arafat was invited to deliver a historical speech. Thereafter, the PLO gained an observer status seat in the UN General Assembly.

My first experience affiliating with Fatah started at the age of 12, right after my failed trip to Syria along with my friends. Fatah had an underground organization in Lebanon. One of my schoolteachers was one of its local leaders. They were meeting secretly to plan their activities in Lebanon, but the Lebanese secret police had them under surveillance, so they used me and a friend of mine to pass messages between them. We also took bags full of papers, which were the minutes of their secret meetings, and set them on fire somewhere in an open area away from buildings and people. This continued until 1969.

I was 13 when Palestinian fighters established bases in the south of Lebanon, close to the borders of Palestine. During this same period, secret Fatah activists in the refugee camps smuggled weapons into all Palestinian refugee camps in Lebanon. When the time was right, they declared an armed uprising by taking over the camps and kicking out the Lebanese police, which had the worst possible reputation for oppressing Palestinians. I was walking the streets that day and saw Fidayeen with their Kalashnikovs (AK-47s) and other light and medium-grade weapons all around. It felt like a day of liberation, even though it was only the liberation of refugee camps. It felt as though people finally took matters in their own hands. The liberation movement finally arrived for the Palestinians in Lebanon, and pride and hope arrived with it.

Shortly after, I joined the ranks of the young recruits in the refugee camps and surroundings neighborhoods. Like my peers, I volunteered, attended regular meetings, and underwent military training. Training included climbing a rope tied 20 feet high from the ground, between two sides of a street, with tires set on fire below. We were required to crawl on the rope from one end to the other. Falling into the fire would've proved disastrous. A couple of youngsters lost their grip on the rope and landed in the fire, but were rescued before the flames caused them serious burns. Training was very difficult at times, especially while jumping over obstacles and crawling on the ground. Some trainers were shooting real bullets between us as some kind of preparation for a real battle, and occasionally, some trainees actually got hit and wounded. All that conformed to the ideas

Fatah brought with it. I felt the pride that was created in the atmosphere among my people, and Palestine felt much closer.

Influence of popular and successful revolutions like that of China under Mao Tse-tung, Vietnam, and others in other areas of the world served as models to be followed. In a short period of time, Beirut, in particular, and most of Lebanon, became an open ground for the Palestinian revolution. "Popular liberation movement" was a term commonly used and believed in. Palestinians believed their popular liberation movement would grow and become victorious. I dreamt that such a movement would, one day, be understood and accepted by the Israelis themselves. Other smaller movements influenced by the communist parties believed that somehow, the labor class of the Israelis and Palestinians would someday unite and together create a new social and political movement, which would lead to the creation of a secular socialist state in Palestine with equal rights, granted to all its citizens. All these ideas and outlooks were floating around, and some young people believed in them. Similar to thousands of young Palestinian revolutionary recruits, I went about my new political and military training passionately; we believed we were heroes in the making.

Arafat with Fatah Fighters in the mid 1960s

Chapter 5

PLO, from Jordan to Lebanon

Palestinian fighters became well settled in the south of Lebanon. They established their bases in mountain caves, narrow enclaves, and had support offices in the villages nearby, which were mostly inhabited by Lebanese Shia Muslims. The Shia sect is the second-largest sect in Islam after the Sunni sect. Most people of South Lebanon saw hope in the Palestinian fighters and supported them in many ways. After all, these villagers had experienced many years of abandonment and indifference by the Lebanese government. They were ruled by traditional Shiite leaders who belonged to feudal families, misusing their power over the villagers who were mostly farmers and peasants.

In 1970, the Palestinian movement with its leadership in Jordan had a major conflict with King Hussein, who saw in the new movement a threat to his own regime. The majority of Jordan's population was Palestinian. Jordan, theoretically, could have turned into a de facto Palestinian state at the time. Leaders of the Palestinian national movement were much less-experienced politicians compared to the king, who had formed strong alliances with the greatest Western states and regional powers. The Palestinian revolution in Jordan also gave the king's regime many pretexts to assemble strong support against the chaos created by Palestinian factions. Palestinian factions stationed in most neighborhoods became the day-to-day ruling power and thereby undermined the authority of the king and his government. Whether the Palestinian leadership intended it or not, a state within a state was in place. The PLO democracy between its factions was very lax in enforcing its rules of conduct, unlike traditional militaries or governments. It was unable to control or discipline unruly militants, so every faction was a semi-independent power, "Democracy in a jungle of arms" was a famous phrase Yasser Arafat used to often proudly describe the democracy of the PLO. It was that jungle environment which created ill feelings among many sectors of the people in Jordan, and the king seized that sentiment, while he obtained the support of the United States and other countries to wage a war aimed to expel the PLO and its forces from Jordan. Luckily for the Palestinian leaders and fighters, they received help from the Syrians to relocate to Lebanon, particularly the south of Lebanon, and thereafter to Beirut, the capital, and then to most of the Lebanese cities, except for the areas which were mostly inhibited by Christian Lebanese, whose majority were not supportive of the Palestinian faction's move of operations and headquarters into Lebanon.

Christian parties grew ever more resentful of the Palestinians and made it clear early on. They made their presence known by friction with the Palestinians on every possible occasion. They did not want the Palestinians to get too comfortable and reinforce their grip on the country as they viewed it. It would threaten their historically rooted power and superiority to all other religious sects of Lebanon. The reality of the matter is that the Palestinians never planned to replace anyone and never wanted to become citizens of Lebanon or Jordan. All they wanted was a home for their national resistance movement, and since no country was going to provide such a home voluntarily, they had to use their force to secure it. They wanted to fight Israel; they wanted to make Israel unsettled and uncomfortable in their homeland while they were displaced and refugees wandering the earth.

Modeling after successful liberation movements, they knew they needed a strong base. The presence of such a base was a threat that the political regimes of Jordan and Lebanon could not tolerate. An alliance of PLO factions with local opposition parties in these two countries was rightfully thought to be a major factor which would change the status quo. The PLO tried hard to avoid confrontation, however, despite all assurances the PLO leadership tried to provide to the Lebanese traditional leadership, just like it tried to do in Jordan before that, they never succeeded, and for good reasons. Contradictions in the Palestinian approach to these matters brought about its failure. So while Arafat offered assurances, George Habash, founding leader of the Popular Front for the Liberation of Palestine, PFLP, the second-largest Palestinian faction, called for revolutionary change of all the Arab pro-Western regimes.

In the end, the regime of King Hussein of Jordan was never a serious fighter against Israel. The king wanted to survive in power and create stability for his state. In Lebanon, particularly most of the Christian Maronite political leadership, they had the same point of view. The Palestinian resistance then, for sure, was meant to face the same problems in different forms, and it was even much more difficult in Lebanon, in spite of a great deal of support by Lebanese national and Pan-Arab parties with everything they could offer, including their own lives. These were the same parties which wanted to eliminate the religious sectarian regime of Lebanon and replace it with a secular democratic form of government. Their alliance with the PLO placed them and the PLO in confrontation with those who wanted to keep and protect the Lebanese religiously structured political regime.

The difference between the Palestinian resistance era in Jordan and that of Lebanon was very significant. In Jordan, the Palestinian resistance found a home due to sympathetic demographics, a population which was and continues to be largely Palestinian. Conversely, in Lebanon, the Palestinian resistance found itself mixed up in a big mess of a few communities strongly divided along religious lines. Many conflicts existed between them, sometimes dormant, but most of the time active. When it was calm, it was like an inactive volcano. While it looked calm on the surface, it was full of fire underneath and ready to explode. The Palestinian resistance in Lebanon was operating against the odds and treading in rough waters. People of the camps knew it but still lived with the hope their resistance was growing and that someday, it would take them back to Palestine. Meanwhile, they regained respect and maintained armed forces strong enough to keep them well positioned and taken seriously. They did not want the times of Lebanese police oppression and discrimination to return. They wanted to live a decent and dignified life until the ultimate goal of return to Palestine was achieved.

The generation of Nakba was most affected by watching their families' ill-fated trip out of Palestine. Very few of them had the luxury of time to reflect on what happened. Most who had jobs were busy trying to mitigate the problems of their families, and the unemployed tried to get visas to travel to another country to find work. The broadest base of revolution came from the younger brothers and sisters who were born in the countries of refuge and became fighters at a young age. Many of them became Shahid, martyrs in military confrontations with the Israeli army, either on the borders or when they infiltrated into Palestine. The Palestinian revolution was conducting what was known as guerilla warfare (small and fragmented groups of fighters) against the newly created state of Israel. Most of them had high morals and high spirits. They believed the revolution would grow and victory would eventually come.

Although I was a very good student at the time, I started losing interest in what school had to offer. Somehow, school started becoming less significant for me and most of my friends. Being part of the revolution made me feel grown, more mature, more powerful than even my teachers at school. Kids like me became young men too soon. We were feared by the school authority and by people on the street. It came to a point that we controlled when the school was to shut down for the day or if political events justified a strike. This very same generation which started out with the belief that academic education was fundamental to the future changed, and suddenly, education of the revolution became much more important. Many dropped out and became full-time informal soldiers, community activists or political operatives of the resistance. The revolution became a way of life, more important than pursuing serious education and future careers. Financial support offered by the PLO factions to all their members contributed to scale down the level of enthusiasm for academic education for a number of young men and women.

In 1971, the PLO rebuilt its strength as a major player in the region. Hostilities in the form of intelligence warfare were going on between the PLO and the king of Jordan (aftershocks of the

September 1970 battles between the two parties). Many atrocities were committed against Palestinians and became known as the September Massacres. King Hussein did not relinquish a claim to the West Bank, which he ruled for almost 20 years after the creation of Israel. Equally important was the claim to custodianship of Jerusalem, particularly, Al-Aqsa, one of three holiest Islamic shrines. To be an Al-Aqsa guardian is a status of magnificent importance, especially since the king's family are descendants of Bani Hashim, the tribe which Prophet Muhammad was born among.

In Lebanon, within a relatively short period of time, an alliance led by Yasser Arafat was created. It was a coalition of Palestinian factions, Lebanese local and Pan-Arabs, leftists, communists, and socialist parties. The alliance controlled the major Lebanese cities and countryside, short of the hardcore Christian enclave of East Beirut, the mountainous area occupied by mostly Maronite Christians, and a part of the coastal area north of Beirut. Lebanon also became a zone which leftist and revolutionary movements from different parts of the world utilized as a safe haven, protected by PLO factions, groups from Ireland, Germany, Africa, Japan, Italy, and Iran while under the late Shah. All set up shops in Lebanon and operated from there. Meanwhile, Fatah and other PLO factions operated out of Southern Lebanon and launched military strikes against Israel, which, in turn, retaliated by bombing Palestinian bases and refugee camps as well. At that time, world media did not use satellite live coverage. Bombs considered illegal to use by the international community in wars were indeed used on Palestinian targets, like the napalm bombs, cluster bombs, and other kinds. Civilian casualties on the Palestinian side were tragic; however, morale of the long-term struggle was high.

PLO factions retaliated and struck back, including at civilian targets in Israel, which satisfied vengeful sentiments, however, they mostly served to be used by the Israeli and Western media to portray the Palestinian struggle as that of vicious terrorists. The PLO did not win much sympathy or support in Western Europe or the United States. On the contrary, Israel's image was successfully further displayed as victims of terrorism.

The PLO leadership did not adopt a strategy of adherence to fighting soldier to soldier only. Casualties were one Israeli to many Palestinians, still, Palestinians were blamed for the violence. Civilian victims prevented the emergence of a peaceful coexistence movement which already exists among both parties of the conflict. Bridges between the two people could not be built. While the PLO called for a secular democratic state for Muslims, Jews, and Christians, its implementation on a daily basis just did not reconcile with its principles and goals. Even the interpretation of the PLO charter was left to mean that it stands for the liquidation of the "Zionist entity, militarily and politically . . . etc." That phrasing diverted focus from the beliefs of young revolutionaries at the time, like me, who aspired for a democratic, secular state for all its citizens. That phrase only served to feed negative media coverage of the PLO in a major way. The PLO contributed to its negative image in the West and other parts of the world by leaving that article of its charter unchanged. The PLO considered Zionism a racist, ethnic-cleansing-motivated movement; however, the PLO did not consider people of the Jewish faith to be enemies of the Palestinian people based on their religion. The PLO failed to properly express how it differentiated between Zionism and Jewish people.

No matter what an enemy does, an oppressed people must not resort to the same methods when it comes to human values. Ultimately, it is better to sacrifice and show a better example. That's easier said than done!!! True, however, this is where a historic leadership paves the way to a much better future. The Palestinian leadership did not perform with such a vision in mind. To convince people that it's better to witness the enemy kill some of their innocent civilians and not do the same to the enemy is a very difficult task. However, it is a task that can make the oppressed prevail and add value to humanity.

In Lebanon, the president who was and had to be a Maronite Christian based on the Lebanese constitutional covenant, along with the Maronite political factions, were getting fed up watching the Alliance of the Palestinians and national leftist parties grow in power, influence, and territorial control. Having had national identity issues, political Maronite factions did not identify themselves as being Arabs. They believed their origins go back to the Phoenicians, even though many history books identify Phoenicians as Canaanites who resided in the coastal part of Syria, Lebanon, and Palestine; yet, they still claimed the Phoenician heritage exclusively.

The Maronite sect originated in the northern part of Syria in AD 410, close to the Byzantine border at the time in Antioch. The name is derived from a priest Maroon, who had certain teachings and a way of life based on worship in solitude. They were persecuted by the Byzantine church in Constantinople mainly over differences between Monophysitism (one nature of Christ, divine-human) versus Chalcedonian (two full natures, one human, one divine nature of Christ), a belief the Maronites held. The Maronites took the high, isolated, and distant mountains of Lebanon as their hideout to survive and spread their message among the people of Lebanon in that area. They were surrounded by a Muslim majority in Lebanon, Syria, and Palestine. Their past persecution by the Byzantines gave them a good cause to be defensive. They entrenched themselves in their enclave.

In Lebanon, religious civil wars took place a couple of times in recent history. In 1860, a civil war broke out between Christians and Druze Lebanese in the mountains where both populations lived. Over ten thousand people were reportedly killed, and many massacres took place. In 1958, another crisis erupted, mostly along religious lines, even though the bigger picture of that conflict was between the Pan-Arabs supporting Gamal Abdel Nasser of Egypt, and the Western right-wing Christian (mainly Maronite) political factions. The conflict was bloody. People had guns on the streets. The situation was wrapped up, especially after the intervention of the United States, by sending marines into Lebanon to support the president at the time, Camille Chamoun, who tried to seek another term which was strongly opposed by a great majority of the people of Lebanon. Finally, he was allowed to finish his term and a more respected general whose policies were more acceptable to the people was elected. His name was Fuad Chehab.

Lebanon survived by coexistence between the Lebanese Muslims who are also divided by three sects, Sunni, Shia, and Druze, and Christians, who are also divided between Maronite, Roman Orthodox, and Catholics. Other Christians live in Lebanon like Armenians. They live in the mostly Christian-populated eastern side of Beirut and the mountains.

During times of peace, the Lebanese are a fun-loving people, known in the Middle East for their much-admired way of life. They are exceptionally clever in business and trade on an international level. Lebanese food is famous and appreciated throughout the world. Lebanese people love to dress fashionably and know how to party. Lebanon has a great tourism industry. However, history has shown during times of civil conflicts a great many massacres were committed based on hatred of the religious beliefs of others. Yet, peace and coexistence has found its way through it all, and Lebanon's beloved character came back.

Even today, underlying tensions continue to exist. Family dynasties have existed for centuries. They were the leaders of their communities by inheritance, and somehow, their power grew when it was correlated to heightened tensions between the different Lebanese populations. Lebanon seems to struggle slowly to do away with religious-political feudalism and move toward democracy, equal rights, and civil liberties without religious discrimination.

Meanwhile, in the late sixties, the PLO political and military new presence at the time was considered a scale-tilting factor, in favor of the Lebanese progressive national parties and movements, which were referred to as the leftists. These parties were in the opposition of the Lebanese regime which was made up of right-wing, religious-based parties, and prominent political families of almost all religious sectors of Lebanon. Kamal Jumblatt, a Druze leader, despite belonging to a political, religious family dynasty, was well respected as progressive, a

Pan-Arab, and Palestinian supporter. He rose to be the leader of the Lebanese national left coalition allied with the PLO and called for abolishing the religious structure of the Lebanese regime. On the other side, the Maronite Christian political leadership went searching for even more powerful allies, Arab, American, European . . . It did not matter. They just wanted to build a military and political body to counter any expansion of the PLO and its Lebanese alliance. They discovered Israel to be the most forthcoming to help. Together, they viewed the PLO as an existential threat. Israel benefited greatly by having the PLO fight on Lebanese soil with any party other than its forces and divert their attention away from Israel. Both sides of the Lebanese political equation were adding and training paramilitary recruits, buying and piling up weapons from every source possible.

Christian right militias made their presence known early on. In 1970, a Palestinian fighter was killed in a battle with an Israeli force. His body was carried in a car caravan funeral from Beirut to Syria. The caravan was ambushed in the town of Kahale. The road to Damascus passes right through the town. Lebanese Christian right-wing militias killed and injured many Palestinians. It was the first aggressive act of a large magnitude, with no apparent reason whatsoever, other than the fact that they wanted to pick a fight with the PLO. This incident did not escalate and no retaliation took place, despite the anger which swept through the Palestinian communities in Lebanon. They remained restrained.

PLO factions enhanced their presence militarily and politically. They provided community services to the refugees, particularly with jobs and medical services. Many Lebanese community leaders who were not fond of the Lebanese political system allied themselves to a great degree with the PLO. Most of them had a direct relationship with Yasser Arafat, the PLO chairman who was a man of distinguished charm and who knew how to attract supporters. He supported them and protected them. Arafat had a magnetic charisma contrary to the image created and depicted by the Western media. He was loved, honored, and respected by the great majority of the Palestinian people everywhere, including those who differed with his views and leadership style.

In 1969, an agreement was reached in Egypt between Arafat and the Lebanese army commander Emile Bustani, sponsored by President Nasser, which became known as "The Cairo Agreement." The parties agreed that the PLO forces' presence in Southern Lebanon was acceptable. It also organized the relationship between the Lebanese army, government, and the PLO, and the agreement also recognized the PLO jurisdiction over the population of the Palestinian refugee camps in Lebanon and the PLO leadership quarter mainly in an area called the "Fakahani quarter." It lasted, however, just a little over 2 years, when tensions between the Lebanese army units and one of the PLO factions escalated, resulting in the Lebanese army units circling the refugee camps in April 1973. I was barely 16, attending school in a Beirut southern suburb, when gunfire erupted and explosions occurred. The school became chaotic. The principal simply decided to dismiss us to go home . . . except for one problem: The school was located in a neighborhood outside a Palestinian refugee camp called Bourj el-Barajneh, and a great many students, including myself, lived a few miles away in Sabra and Shatila refugee camps. Public transportation was halted, cars raced by, people ran in the streets . . . Everyone was trying to get to his or her home and make sure their family members were safe. I was confused about where to go. I thought maybe going into the Bourj refugee camp was a good idea. At least I would be between Palestinians and find some protection among Fatah comrades.

I walked into the camp, got to Fatah offices, and saw volunteer militia fighters. They were hardly organized. They were just exchanging news and passing rumors back and forth. When someone came and joined them and told stories of what he saw, especially news of fighters on the front line only a few hundred meters away, and of those who blew up an army carrier, or better yet, an army tank, that was followed by naming one of the Palestinian fighters getting injured, one guy who was standing among us then heard his brother's name mentioned as killed. He had become a "Shahid." This man totally lost control. He was carrying a Kalashnikov, unlocked the safety handle, pushed another handle which made the rifle ready to shoot, and shouted he was going to kill the bastards who killed his brother. Off he ran to the battlefront.

I stayed in that place about 2 hours. The gunfire and explosions only got louder and were continuous. My hopes of a cease-fire faded away. I then decided to walk home. I got out of the camp and went to the main street toward my school again. Luckily, that area was overpopulated with civilians, and the army did not get into it. I walked a couple of kilometers, got close to the outskirts of Shatila refugee camp, and right there, I saw an army tank totally burned and destroyed. The closer I got to streets where army and PLO fighters were facing each other, the more deserted were the streets.

I managed to get close to a neighborhood which is located between our home in Sabra and the Shatila camp. Between that neighborhood and me was the main road to the airport, and the army was all over it. I just decided to make a run for it and hoped I didn't get shot while crossing it. I raced over the road, aware of every fraction of every second as I did so, and I got to the other side in one piece. The rest of the road was relatively safer, given that the Lebanese army did not shell civilian-populated areas. I made it home safe and sound, but this was the first time in my life I got so close to an actual gun battle and was in the middle of live explosions and war damage. I was frightened by the 500 millimeter fast automatic guns constantly being fired.

The fight went on and escalated every day, with more and more shelling. The army air force took part in the fight, however, looking back, and to be fair, the Lebanese army did not utilize its full force and did not actually mean to crush the PLO, or at least, did not seriously try to do it. I am not really sure whether the president of Lebanon meant to do that, or he just was under tremendous pressure domestically and from many other Arab governments and presidents, like Syria, Egypt, and possibly Saudi Arabia, during that time. The PLO enjoyed very good relationships with all three of those countries, in addition to the popular support of the PLO by Arab masses.

A cease-fire was declared, the army retreated back to their barracks, and the PLO and its different factions were back operating with a lot of flexibility. It was obvious to everyone who lived in Beirut during these years that the PLO's, despite denying it was a state within a state, jurisdiction was not only the Palestinians, it actually spread its influence among the Lebanese communities in the areas it controlled, whether in the capital or in cities and villages, particularly in southern Lebanon, Sidon, Tyre, as well as most of the southern towns and villages. They were under control of the PLO and its Lebanese allies. Large numbers of Lebanese were enrolled or involved somehow with the PLO. Many young men and women, mostly Muslim Shia, were fighters and activists; many other Sunni Moslems and Christians were also involved.

The Palestinian cause was an emotional one which attracted young and romantic freedom fighters from around the Arab world and many other parts of the world. I once encountered a young man from

Tunisia walking the street in Sabra. He stopped me to tell me he came from his country on his own to volunteer with the Palestinians to help liberate Palestine. They came by the hundreds, if not thousands, to endanger their lives for the sake of the Palestinian cause. Many of them were killed in battles. I had a good Egyptian friend, Mahmoud was his name, a young Syrian, who I witnessed being shot in the abdomen while ironically fighting the Syrian army on the outskirts of Sabra. Luckily, he survived. Lebanese young men and women fought against the Lebanese army and the Christian right militias when clashes took place. Some died and were buried in the Martyrs' Cemetery, while others who infiltrated into Palestine and were killed were buried in what is known as the Cemeteries of Numbers, in Israel. They are cemeteries with graves that don't have name plates, only numbers assigned to the buried bodies. I don't know if the Israelis have identified them all and kept their identity records to match the numbers.

The PLO leadership at all levels did not learn much from their Jordanian experience. They repeated the same behavior and never managed to create a disciplinary system to restrain their activists from practicing undue authority, which, most of the time, individually motivated the misuse and abuse of power against both Lebanese and Palestinian ordinary people. Their property and business were not respected. It was not a common behavior or an overwhelming phenomena, but the small minority which misbehaved was enough to spoil the PLO image all over. Complaints were received by the leadership, including Yasser Arafat, however, no real remedy came about to eliminate or even significantly minimize such behavior of individuals, groups, and sometimes a whole faction of the PLO.

The PLO had no real disciplinary judicial body, or a sort of military police, or even a specialized civilian police. It was all mixed up. Anyone with a gun could act to police the people if he chose to. He could do it no matter if he was right or wrong. During the same time, there were groups and volunteers who did community work. They helped people, tried to meet their needs. They were educated and showed a true love for the people, but somehow, the voice of chaos was stronger. Arafat and his leadership tried to compensate through daily crisis management and problem solving, as problems always occurred, and that only kept them chasing negative events, rather than put a system in place to address the reasons which caused them. I heard ordinary Lebanese citizens complain about being ruled by "those Palestinians." Resentment was building up, and these problems were mostly ignored and unaddressed in any systematic way by the PLO.

In the summer of 1972, I, along with four other friends, was sent to Syria for military training. It was not a normal trip. We were taken through the borders with special permits all the way to a small military camp on the outskirts of Damascus, where, I remember, my friends and I, along with the trainers, were the only ones with no kaffiyeh (the traditional Palestinian men's headdress) covering our heads and faces. All other trainees were completely masked. We did not meet any of them, or even speak to them. We had our own trainer, and it was arranged for trainees not to mix. Later, I came to know those masked men arrived from Palestine, to train and go back to join the underground resistance against the Israelis. I was almost 16 at the time. Trainers were shooting rockets and blowing up explosives all daylong. They were confident and superaccurate.

It was during that trip, Amer, one of my friends, recognized a Fatah fighter who used to be stationed in Beirut, a few yards from Amer's home. Amer said hello, and that was it. Then Amer leaned toward me and said, "This is the guy who shot three young guys, killing two of them during a dispute over flirting with a girl. I was close by when that incident happened. I heard the shooting, then saw three bloody guys carried away to a hospital. Two of them died, and the man who shot them disappeared. Many were told he was in a jail, being tried, etc." It was during that trip that I saw him, free as a bird. He was transferred from Beirut to Damascus. This was how some serious issues were dealt with. The PLO was a mixed bag; mostly good, some bad, and some just plain ugly. Unfortunately for the good, the bad and the ugly caused a lot of damage. It was a very complex structure, meant to be inclusive. It was inclusive. It included the very honest, sincere volunteer, to the very dirty, self-serving users and abusers of the cause. With no significant rules in place to govern them and no policing force to keep them from acting like authoritarian rulers, some were no better than organized criminal groups. They used their membership in the PLO to commit crimes, like extorting money for protection of businesses in the Hamra and Zaytuneh districts in Beirut, where many bars with prostitutes were located. Others were engaged in selling weapons and drugs. Even mafia-style assassinations were carried out for territorial control.

My father's uncle was in his seventies when two of the known organized group members decided to steal his car and drove it away. My father's uncle came to tell me about it. I went to the Fatah security commander and brought my father's uncle with me and he told him his story. A meeting was arranged between the commander, Imad, a ruthless man, and me. From the outset of the meeting, the commander said, "This car belongs to Osama's uncle" (Osama is my nickname).

Imad said, "Oh, so the car now has owners."

I answered, "Imad, do you know of any car out there that does not have an owner?"

He said, "Well, I spent money on the car and am not giving it back without getting reimbursed."

I said, "Why would you spend money on a car which is not yours to begin with?"

He said, "Well, this is the way it is. You get me my money, or I will just drive it into the sea, and you'll never see the car again."

I looked toward the commander, who concluded the meeting and told Imad to leave and that he would contact him later. The commander said to me, "Listen, they will drive the car into the sea, and they can also hurt your old relative. Just give them the money, get the car back, and get it over with."

I went to my father's uncle, collected 2,000 Lebanese liras (about $600 at the time), delivered the money the next day, and the car was delivered to me by Ahmad, another well-known organized group member, with an almost empty gas tank. I filled the car with some gas and drove it to my old relative, who was happy to see his car back. This is an example of how these guys did business on a daily basis. I must add that was a peaceful transaction for them and us. Many other transactions were not so peaceful, and often, someone got hurt in the process.

In the middle of 1973, I was sent along with the same group of friends, Muhannad, Fakhri, Nidal, Jareer, and Amer, to South Lebanon, to an area called Al-Arqoub. It was also commonly known as "Fatah land" and was referred to as such in the international media and political circles. It is in an area between rocks and fertile soil. It is also quite hilly and has many caves in the rocks. Fatah's elite fighters, the Nusur Al-Arqoub in Arabic (Eagles of Al-Arqoub) were based in that area.

Our group was broken into smaller units of two, then taken to a station and we lived with a group of five fighters in one medium-size tent hidden in a shallow cave well camouflaged under trees, in order to be invisible to Israeli air force surveillance spy planes which were very often in the skies, attempting to spot those fighters known for their courage, fierce fighting, and above all, who were well trained and experienced. Fakhri and I were one unit. We lived, cooked, ate, and took night shift guard duties when other fighters slept.

We spent about 2 weeks there, made good friends, practiced shooting in the wild open areas, took long mountain hikes, listened to the fighters' stories, their battles, even funny stories like one fighter who came from Iraq. He was a Kurd, well built and very strong. His comrades told the story of how he and his big German shepherd dog walked and walked during a battle when fighters were maneuvering to relocate and disappear from direct confrontation with Israeli units, which outnumbered them. The Israelis had far more advanced weaponry. The Kurd fighter's dog got exhausted way before the fighter, despite being a big dog, so the fighter carried him on his shoulders on top of carrying his own weapon and equipment, and continued the long trek. His strength for doing that became famous amongst the fighters.

One night, dogs barked so loud, fighters took positions not knowing who was nearby, until they heard a man's voice calling one of the fighters' name and asking him to control his dogs. All the fighters laughed. It was the top commander of Nusur Al-Arqoub. He was referred to as Comrade Naeem, known to be talented in guerilla warfare, honest, and brave. We spent a good part of the night drinking tea and listening to his views about the Palestinian revolution, both political and military. He was a very idealistic man. A couple of years later during the civil war, he was kidnapped, never be heard from again, while on a boat in the Mediterranean between Beirut and the Northern Lebanese city of Tripoli, where he was heading with Hanna Mikahail (Abu Omar), a well respected Fatah leader and thinker, and a group of their comrades to lead the defense of the city from the Christian right-wing forces and their allies at the time the Syrian army.

Chapter 6

October War, 1973, and Peace Settlement Prospects

October 6, 1973. It was the tenth day of the holy month of Ramadan. Most people were fasting. The whole neighborhood was relatively quiet except for shoppers for the evening meal which breaks the fasting. Praying was heard on the loudspeakers which were hung on top of the mosque minarets. Merchants were happy during that time, because people shopped for everything—more food, sweets for desserts, and, more important, people bought clothes and toys for children to celebrate the Eid at the end of the fasting month. Our fasting as Muslims is truly a painful experience, especially for those who wake up early in the morning to go to work or school, and those mothers who stay home cleaning and cooking while fasting. Muslims are not even allowed to drink a drop of water from sunrise to sunset. We were taught fasting will make us experience how the poor and hungry feel. It makes us appreciate what we have in life, and it trains us to be patient. All these things are true. People are much more spiritual and forgiving during the holy month. Many prayers are heard at night and dawn. Muslims restrain from many pleasures and dedicate themselves much more to worship. Of course, not all Muslims do this. Many can't take it, especially if they are sick, anemic, or simply not disciplined enough to do it. However, they are generally discreet about it, and very respectful to the overall fasting population.

I was walking on Sabra Street, between the street peddlers, small shops, and the large coffeehouses which were usually crowded with the old, retired, and unemployed, playing cards and smoking *arguileh* (Arabic for a hookah water pipe) and cigarettes. Usually, many of them constantly argued about their card game or discussed politics, with a cloud of smoke filling the place, and the waiter running from one table to another with Turkish coffee or a refill of mesquite charcoal for *arguileh*. Sometimes street peddlers with small accessories like cigarette lighters, small knives, and rings in their hands tried to make sales.

Suddenly, everything became quiet except for loud radios blaring nationalistic songs and the voice of a radio announcer. Crowds in groups of almost a hundred people gathered around a radio, listening as the announcer, proud and confident as during previous wars, declared that war just broke out. Egyptian and Syrian forces were advancing to liberate lands occupied by Israel in 1967. A feeling of euphoric pride overtook the Arab masses. Having experienced the disappointment of the 1967 bitter and humiliating defeat, people were very cautious about believing all they heard on the radio. They were looking for any sign of exaggeration of victories or the numbers of Israeli fighter jets downed by Arab armies. During the 1967 war, radio announcers claimed more numbers of Israeli jets were shot down than what the Israeli air force actually possessed. It became a joke for years after. The 1973 war was different. Announcers were much calmer, numbers of losses on both sides sounded more realistic, and people listened to BBC

(British Broadcasting Company) radio, despite not liking its political bias. People thought it was usually more news accurate at the time and necessary to cross-check what Egyptian and Syrian radio broadcasters were saying.

The news from the battlefronts sounded very encouraging for the Arab people. Both Egyptian and Syrian forces were on the offensive, and for the first time ever, the Israeli forces were retreating in defeat. Egyptian special units crossed the Suez Canal covered by over 2,000 artillery guns firing on the Israeli side. Over 250 Egyptian fighter jets and bombers attacked Israeli positions and air force bases. Egyptian fighters by the thousands carried antitank rocket launchers and rendered Israeli tanks ineffective in the battlefield. They crossed over on rubber boats. They also attacked Israeli Bar Lev sand fortifications with high-powered water pipes, and in the darkness of night, Egyptians were successful in installing bridges for their armored vehicles, tanks, and troops which crossed the canal and fortified their positions.

On the Syrian-Israeli front, the Golan Heights were attacked with a similar scenario. Syrian forces advanced by the thousands. Syrian air force and artillery bombarded Israeli forces. Israel, in shock and disbelief, was caught unprepared. American help came quickly with an airlift mission sending battle-ready tanks and weapons into Sinai Desert to compensate for vast losses suffered by the Israelis. SAM antiaircraft surface-to-air missiles proved to be a huge surprise, which crippled Israeli air force jets. They were shot down before they could return to their bases.

Since Lebanon is adjacent to both Syrian and Israeli fronts, I often witnessed what is known as a dogfight between the two sides' fighter jets, and many times, I saw Israeli jets turn and fly away fast, followed by a SAM rocket. Sometimes the jet escaped the missile's range, and other times, it did not make it back to base at all. It took awhile for the Israeli forces to get over the shock, reorganize, and counterattack on both fronts. On the Egyptian side their weak defenses were able to penetrate between the Egyptian armies and circled the 3rd army, and on the Syrian side, the Israelis drove back the Syrian forces, though not to the prewar lines.

By October 22, the United Nations arranged a cease-fire between the fighting armies. However, the war was, by all expert opinions, a great Egyptian-Syrian, and therefore, Arab, victory. For the first time since Palestine was occupied, Arab masses felt the victory. Pride was restored, and people believed that Arabs were not doomed to failure. They could finally connect with the glory of the past when Arabs were able to defend their national rights; indeed, defended their lands, and their own soldiers liberated it, by utilizing their own commitment and creativity. Of course, victory would not have been possible had it not been for Soviet support, both military and political. The two superpowers of the time actually went on nuclear alert while watching closely how far that war was going. Given that Israel was already a nuclear power, no one could know what the Israelis might have done if their army collapsed on the battlefronts. The Palestinians felt they were on top of the world. Finally, luck was moving their way!

Peace Settlement and Compromises

It was not too long before political initiatives were thrown on the diplomatic tables, offered by the United States, Europe, and the Soviets. All were trying to broker new peace talks. During that time, the Palestinian leadership was being approached and pressured to compromise in order for the PLO to be taken seriously by the world powers.

Shortly after the 1973 war, Palestinian factions were showing more strength, launched many attacks across the borders into Israeli northern settlements close to the Lebanese borders, and the Israeli air force retaliated by bombing many Palestinian fighter bases and the civilian areas surrounding them. Many people were displaced from their homes, in addition to the loss of lives. People of the south were tired of having to carry the cost of the Palestinian-Israeli ongoing war. Even the more supportive section of the Lebanese people showed signs of growing unhappiness with the escalating conflict in their land. They felt they contributed much more than their fair share in supporting the Palestinian cause, while their control on their sovereignty was diminishing daily. Israel and the Palestinians were calling the shots. They were just caught in the middle and did not know where that was leading them. The Lebanese Christian right parties became more nervous and felt the Palestinian threat grew much larger, and so did the threat from Palestinian Lebanese allies. The race to acquire weapons and growing paramilitary forces peaked and tensions between the two sides of the Lebanese political equation were on the rise.

Meanwhile, Palestinian leadership set itself on the track of political compromise. In 1974, and as a huge boost of the PLO by the Arab League of states, they met in Morocco. The PLO was recognized as the sole legitimate representative of the Palestinian people and was given almost a full state status membership in the league, to the displeasure of Jordan's King Hussein, who was still, by then, hoping to regain the West Bank for his kingdom. The new PLO status paved the way to a much-larger event which took place on the international arena, an invitation by the United Nations General Assembly to Yasser Arafat, where he delivered a historic speech, followed by recognition by the United Nations of the PLO as a

Palestinian people's representative with an observer member seat. It was a year of great success for the PLO, on its way to legitimize its existence and establish a diplomatic presence in many countries. Previously, some countries hesitated to recognize the organization, but no longer since the PLO had now gained United Nations' legitimacy, although some allies of Israel, namely the United States, Western Europe, and other countries neither recognized the PLO, nor had direct contact with the organization. The event was a historical turning point, at which the Palestinian leadership believed establishing a Palestinian state was within close range. Some of them even thought it was going to happen within 5 years.

The encouraged PLO launched a full-scale diplomatic outreach. It was desperately seeking recognition of the U.S. and its Western allies, which, if secured, the leadership thought would pressure Israel to negotiate and reach a settlement over the conflict. During that time, moderate Palestinian leaders were encouraged and supported, while the militant leaders were being weakened.

As a young student activist, I was more idealistic, and, therefore, more sympathetic to those I believed were more loyal to the Fatah covenant, which called for a democratic secular state for all of historical Palestine, with equal rights for all its citizens. The covenant also called for "destruction of the Zionist entity," taken by most to mean the "destruction of Israel." Such statements were very harmful to the Palestinian cause. They just played on Palestinian anger, but certainly did not gain new friends for the Palestinian cause. Palestinian leadership of the time was not visionary when it came to this issue. I wonder how events would have changed if they did not have such a phrase and only called for one state for all its citizens and no discrimination based on religion, even if that looked only like a dream.

While Zionist leaders considered the PLO a terrorist organization, Zionism was, on the other hand, considered a racist movement, even by international standards. A resolution numbered 3379 of the United Nations General Assembly was adopted on November 10, 1975, and considered Zionism as a form of racism and racial discrimination, then later that was repealed by another resolution on December 17, 1991, a time in which the U.S and its allies had the strongest influence in the UN, one of the results of the end of the cold war.

The notion that a Jew is a Zionist was fundamentally rejected by the Palestinians. The Zionism movement claims to be the national movement of the Jewish people to achieve their dream of a homeland and their own state. It somehow wants the world to believe that if not all, then most, Jewish people are Zionists. The biggest conflict with Zionism for me, was and continues to be, that for it to exist as defined by its founders, and flourish, we the Palestinians have to die as a nation. Who can accept such a proposal? Would any nation, people, or even a tribe agree to it? Zionism took over a homeland with entire cities, towns, villages, fields, and a society which existed for thousands of years, simply claiming there was never a state of Palestine, so therefore, there is no Palestine or Palestinians, because God promised the land a few thousand years ago to the Jewish people. They were pushed out after, and are now back to claim it, even though Jewish people were spread out during those past few thousand years across the globe.

In Herzl's book *The Jewish State*, he states, "Palestine is our unforgettable historic homeland . . . Let me repeat once more my opening words: The Jews who will it shall achieve their State. We shall live at last as free men on our own soil, and in our own homes peacefully die. The world will be

117

liberated by our freedom, enriched by our wealth, magnified by our greatness. And whatever we attempt there for our own benefit will redound mightily and beneficially to the good of all mankind." He also said, "It depends on the Jews themselves whether this political document remains for the present a political romance. If this generation is too dull to understand it rightly, a future, finer, more advanced generation will arise to comprehend it. The Jews who will try it shall achieve their State; and they will deserve it."

For the Jewish people to go back to a land where they were a couple of thousand years ago is fine. I can accept this much; however, going back and uprooting whoever was there is not fine at all. I can never accept this. It is clear Zionism from its inception is not just calling for a Jewish homeland, for a homeland can be for different people, races, and religions. A state is for everyone with equal rights. Herzl called for a Jewish state, without care for who was already there at the time—a million or more people, descendants of people who have been there for thousands of years. Maybe Palestinians just disburse. After all, they are Arabs and can live anywhere in the Arab world, as Jewish Israeli leaders so openly and loudly claimed. Most famous was Golda Meir. She also claimed, "There is no

Palestine people. There are Palestinian refugees."
(She said this in the *New York Times* on January 14,
1976.) As simple as that. How can Zionism claim to
be the savior of the Jewish nationhood and not take
responsibility for the destruction of the Palestinian
nationhood when it denies their existence? Israeli
propaganda claimed Palestinians decided to leave,
and since they chose to leave, they can't be allowed
back. How can people of any country not be able to
go back to their homes and homeland? Most of the
world allowed such a ridiculous distortion of
history to take place and supported it by not doing
anything significant about it for many years. No
matter how Palestinians left their homes and
homeland, whether they were scared of rumors or
actual massacres that took place, or any other
reason, the fact remains . . . It is my right and my
kids' right to go to our homeland and go in and out
as we wish. Can any person believe that people just
decide to leave their homeland of thousands of
years in massive numbers to become refugees in
tents elsewhere without some catastrophic event to
precipitate it? Zionist Jewish leaders insisted and
solidly adopted such claims as truths beyond doubt.

The Zionist movement wanted to be known as
Jewish and democratic. Similar to recent demands
by Israeli governments from the Palestinians to

recognize Israel as a Jewish state . . . not just as a state, but more specifically, a *Jewish* state. If it is a Jewish state, what does that make a non-Jewish person in that state? Does he or she suddenly become an alien, or a second-class minority citizen in his homeland and that of his grandfathers and great-grandfathers? Where is the beginning point for peace, given all these existential contradictions between the Zionist movement, and the PLO? Encouraged by the Soviets, as well as moderate Arab regimes, the PLO compromised and came out with the two-state solution, even though there was debate within the Palestinian factions and the disbursed communities on this new controversial proposal.

In Lebanon, while the political and armed conflict was heating up, the early to the mid-1970s were amazing years. It was not strange to Lebanon as small a country as it is, to be going through war, while some people living in it were not affected and lay at the beach! Or partied hard at night! Lebanon, during the first 5 years of the '70s, was full of tourists from everywhere. Most were Arabs from the Gulf states. In addition, many Lebanese and Palestinians worked abroad. Many of them used to drive their fancy cars to Lebanon in the summer. The mountain and beach towns and cities were bustling with activities. Prices for homes and goods went through the roof during the summer because the tourists and the visitors had lots of cash to throw around. Beach resorts, shopping centers, restaurants, cafes, nightclubs, and the famous Casino du Liban were great attractions. The country was a fun place, and everyone who knew about it wanted to spend a summer in Lebanon. A liberal atmosphere was everywhere, I remember seeing women wearing shorts and strolling down the famous upscale Hamra Street with a dog on a leash. For an Arab country that was definitely not customary. Once during a student demonstration I was not part of, but I happened to be on the sidewalk of the street, and two young men and a young woman jumped out of a car and ran together totally nude. It was their expression of contesting a policy. The police chased them, but another car was waiting for them a few yards ahead. They got into it and drove away. Now, that was *totally* out of character in almost any Arab country, but not Beirut though. It was an Arab city with a lot of European lifestyle.

Theater was a big thing. Famous musicals created by the notable Rahbani Brothers, and the legendary singer Fairoz, a woman with a heavenly voice who was loved all over the Arab world took place. Many cultural and political plays were playing. Some became classic. Famous Egyptian singers held great concerts. My friends and I used to spend time at beaches where I would be swimming in the Mediterranean and could hear Fairoz songs played on loudspeakers. Beautiful girls wearing bikinis were all over. You would not know if you were in Beirut or southern France.

As a teenager, I liked living in Beirut and truly enjoyed the environment. These years were the golden times, as none of us knew what lay ahead. Groups of teenagers went to the beach or organized trips on a bus to the mountains where cedar trees thousands of years old decorated the mountaintops, standing majestically partly covered by snow. Only a few driving hours separated the beach and these mountaintops. It was a time where youth, revolution, love, and poetry came together, so very idealistic, yet so real.

Chapter 7

Amid Lebanon's Civil War

A demonstration took place in Sidon, an old city south of Beirut, on February 26, 1975. Maarouf Saad, the city parliament deputy at the time, was among the fishermen demonstrating for their rights, demanding more attention and help from the government. Saad, a popular leader, known for his modest, humble background, fought to prevent a Palestine takeover by the Zionist military forces. He was a Pan-Arabist, a great supporter of Nasser of Egypt, loved by the people of his city and well liked and respected by most Lebanese national and leftist parties. A sniper shot and critically wounded Saad. The sniper was a member of the Lebanese security forces. The incident was considered an assassination. Sidon was in an uproar with strikes, tire burnings, and angry people everywhere. Saad was rushed to a hospital, where he remained in a critical condition and died on March 6, 1975. Blaming the Christian right-wing forces and their supporting government security forces made that assassination a prelude to what happened a month later.

Ain al-Rummaneh Bus Massacre

It was customary at that time for many Palestinian factions to commemorate their special events, the anniversary of their founding, a leaders' martyrdom, and a large-scale military operation against the Israelis. On April 13, 1975, the Popular Front for the Liberation of Palestine-General Command, a supermilitant faction, celebrated a successful attack on Kiryat Shmona, an Israeli settlement town across Lebanese borders. It was usual at the time that a large number of militants and civilians parade the streets of the western, mostly Muslim, side of Beirut. Like many people in my neighborhood, I walked that parade, just being part of a large event, which is why a great many people in those days were part of the crowd—not at all because they really were supporters of the PFLP-GC. Unlike its name, it was not very popular. That day the parade was meant to show support and strength of the PFLP-GC. Competition among Palestinian factions was also common. Many of these factions were created and supported by Arab regimes like Iraq, Syria, and Libya. Somehow, regimes which mostly came to power by coups d'état wanted influence within the PLO, and, if possible, a takeover of the PLO leadership would've been nice. Leaders of these regimes claimed to play a major active role in supporting the Palestinians to liberate their homeland, a cause most Arab people felt passionate about. Other regimes like Saudi Arabia exercised their influence through money and leveraged political support.

April 13, 1975, was a different day in Beirut, Lebanon, and the Arab countries, for it marked the beginning of a new era. After the parade, which ended at the Martyrs' Cemetery on the side of Shatila refugee camp, the crowd disbursed, and the buses loaded people and militants who came from other refugee camps in Lebanon to participate in the event. Buses took off going south, north, and east, back to where they came from. One of those buses carrying approximately 26 people in addition to the driver headed to Tal Zaatar, a Palestinian refugee camp located in the heart of Eastern Beirut, with neighboring suburbs famous as support bases of the Kataeb, the main Christian right-wing militant organization. The bus crossed a mostly Shia neighborhood into Ain al-Rummaneh, a Christian neighborhood with a strong militant presence. Kataeb claimed that a short time before that, gunmen driving fast shot and killed two people in front of a church where Pierre Gemayel, founder and leader of the Kataeb, was supposed to attend a mass. Kataeb considered that an assassination attempt. That story was disputed. Palestinians and Lebanese called it an invention to justify what Kataeb militants committed that same day. They spread out throughout the streets, ambushed the Palestinian bus, showered it with gunfire, and killed everyone on it.

When the news reached the other side of town, it had a chilling effect. People's faces showed fear of what the future may hold. Lebanese security forces went on high alert. They were seen all over the streets which divided communities. Christians and Muslims were not totally segregated in different parts of Beirut or Lebanon. Entire towns and neighborhoods of Christians were surrounded by towns of Muslims. The opposite was true too. Some Muslim towns or neighborhoods were in the middle of Christian towns. These small communities of both sides rightfully feared for their lives. That day people on the streets talked about the bus massacre. Cars filled with people drove fast to get off the streets. People rushed to go home. Grocery stores were crowded with people wanting to buy and store food, as was the case when wars broke out, because people feared food stores would shut down or run out of basic food items.

Suddenly, armed fighters filled the streets. Militants' cars armed with rocket launchers and heavy machine guns were heading to hot spots, and apparently the eastern side of Beirut underwent the same events. Paramilitary forces of Christian right-wing factions on one side, Palestinian and Lebanese national and leftist factions on the other side were facing each other. Shortly after sunset an exchange of gunfire started. It did not stop with any kind of certainty until 15 years later. It took the lives of hundreds of thousands and ethnic-cleansed hundreds of thousands more. And many hundreds of thousands left the country. Thousands fell into poverty, while many warlords and arms dealers, known as merchants of death, became wealthy.

That night, all young and armed men and women reported to their bases in the different Palestinian refugee camps and supporting surrounding areas. In Sabra, we could hear gunfire and explosions taking place between Ain al-Rummaneh and the bordering Shayah, a Shia pro-Palestinian neighborhood on the southeastern side of the city. My friends and I did not know what we were up against. We knew a civil war started, but we did not imagine what it meant or how long it could last. We thought we were going to be the victors, for sure, since we were representing the good. However, we were very naïve and ignorant.

Battles started in that spot and spread to all areas where both sides had guns and supporters to carry them. Beirut skies were filled with flying bullets and gun shells and loud explosions. Some people did not take the first few days seriously, especially those who had needed to go to other side of the city to earn a living. Some of them were not so lucky to get back home. A phenomena emerged called "mobile checkpoint," where a group of Kataeb militants would just randomly make a checkpoint on a street leading to West Beirut. They checked identity cards, not just for a security check, but for the ID cardholder's religion. Lebanese ID cards stated whether the holder was a Muslim or Christian, in addition to other pertinent information which would identify the person. Most of the time a name by itself was enough to identify the person's religion or even sect. Many of those commuters from the West side did not make it back home.

Extremist Kataeb militants introduced horrible ways of killing people once they were identified to be Muslims, and much worse for being a Palestinian. In many cases, bodies were found near trash dumpsters, or on the sides of the streets close to the historic Beirut Museum, which was close to the most western point of the eastern side where the Kataeb and their allies were dug in. Red Cross carried dead bodies and transported them to West Beirut. Bodies were mutilated. Ears, noses, even sexual organs were cut off. Sometimes eyes had been plucked out. Naturally, those actions increased the degree of hatred exponentially. Acts of revenge started on the western side as well; however, these were fewer in comparison with what occurred on the other side.

Years later, I watched a documentary interview with Shimon Peres, president of Israel, who was a minister and prime minister in many Israeli governments. Peres said that he assigned Fuad Ben-Eliezer, an Israeli high-ranking army general, on a mission. He was to visit the Lebanese Kataeb forces, led by Bachir Gemayel, son of the party founder, Pierre Gemayel. The purpose was to assess whether Kataeb could make a reliable ally. Ben-Eliezer reported seeing people tied to car bumpers by ropes and chains and dragged while alive on the streets. When asked who these people were, Bachir Gemayel told him that these were Palestinians captured by his forces.

Israel and the Christian right wing had started contact and a relationship years before . . . Some claim as early as the fifties . . . However, it was kept quiet. At the beginning of 1975, radicals of Kataeb and other Christian right-wing parties showed a great deal of anti-Arab sentiment. They also showed sympathy and support of Israeli policies. Some were very vocal of their contempt of Arab people and often made jokes of their inferiority. Etienne Saqr was a founder and leader of the Guardians of the Cedars militant group. He was well-known for his statement of wanting to kill every Palestinian his group could, and he never differentiated between a civilian or a militant, an adult or a child. It just did not matter to him.

Early on, Israel decided to extend help, arms, logistics, and any other means, and, of course, political and diplomatic support, to the Christian right-wing leadership. They found in Bachir Gemayel their man, who as the future president, would get rid of the Palestinians and lead Lebanon to a peace treaty with Israel.

It did not take long for all the small pockets of Christian and Muslim communities on both sides to empty out. People just left everything mostly to the other side in order to stay with relatives or they rented other homes. Left behind them were their homes, neighbors, and friends they had known since their childhood. It was a sad scene for me to pass through Haret Hurayk, a small Christian neighborhood, located between Sabra, where I lived, and the Beirut southern suburb where my school was located. I used to ride my bicycle to school every day through that neighborhood. It was a special place. I loved passing by the homes, seeing the beautiful roses extending from inside the grounds to over the side of the streets. I passed by the church and remembered when my friends and I used to ditch school and go to that place to hang out or flirt with the girls in the neighboring "Christian Nuns' School for Girls." We had girlfriends in that school. Now the place was too quiet and empty; no people were around. On the other side of the city, the same exact thing happened to Muslim small communities living in Christian-inhabited suburbs. They became terrified and left.

Many cease-fire agreements were declared, only to be broken a day or two later and fighting resumed. For me, all the time during which I was part of Fatah Youth, political education and military training were only an exercise. I did not know that any of it was going to be put to test in a civil war in Lebanon. I thought our energy was going to help liberate Palestine, our homeland. Little did I know a civil war was about to shape our lives day by day. Focus was directed to new enemies. Young men were getting killed by the dozens. Hardly a day passed without a funeral, and sometimes multiple funerals for young men killed on the battlefronts.

With a lot of excitement, courage, and determination, a bunch of young men, including myself, about 15 of us, wanted to be sent to the battlefronts, to fight and defend the revolution from the conspiracy of dissolution. We were sent to Shayah, facing Ain al-Rummaneh. The war was getting closer. It was the first time that the young men who joked and laughed in many meetings had stern faces. We tried hard to hide any expression of fear or confusion as we got closer to the streets ablaze with gunfire and loud explosions. I was sure we all wondered whether one or more of us was going be killed that night. We kept to the sides of the streets, got too close to the other side, and started crossing the street by running fast because a sniper recognized our presence and took shots at us. We were inexperienced in actual battles and quite naïve. That sniper could've had a rocket launcher with an RPG, or a .75 mm gun, which would have torn all of us to shreds. We were lucky. Certainly I was extremely lucky because at one time, when it was my turn to run across the street, while in the middle of the street, a sniper fired a shot, and the bullet flew only inches above my head. I heard it whistle, but my friend actually saw it coming. I ran faster and fell down on the curb of the other side. Abu Bkr, the commander, and a couple of my friends thought I was hit. They shouted my name out loud. I told them I was OK, and a couple of them came to me and helped me up to make sure I was, indeed, unhurt.

The commander did not want to take responsibility for this poorly planned presence on the front lines, so he ordered all of us to start heading back to Sabra. My group managed to fire a few .60 millimeter shells toward the other fighters, wrapped it up, and left. Many other groups fought and fired haphazardly. Of course, there were more organized, more disciplined, and more professional fighting groups on both sides; however, a great part of fighting was done by paramilitary militia volunteers who were not very organized at all. It seemed throughout the civil war, fighters were just shooting with no precise target in mind. They aimed mostly at buildings. Bullets and shells in the thousands hit fronts and sides of every building which happened to be located on the front lines.

We were back in our base, and this was the first time I knew what being in a battlefield meant. Nidal, a young, tall, handsome, and funny guy, was a friend of mine. I met him at the base. We were in the same group. Fakhri, a childhood friend, was also one of our group; Muhannad and Amer as well . . . All high school students except Nidal. He was not going to school. He was a full-time activist. He decided to stay in Shayah and recruited a large number of young Shia Lebanese guys, who were supporters of the Palestinians as most Shia were at the time. He established a base on the forefront of the hot spots where fierce fighting took place. Nidal was a brave guy, and often reckless. When I visited him there, he often dared me to do what he did, which, in my opinion, was crazy. For example, he would carry an RPG on his shoulder, go to the middle of a street—which was a target for many snipers at the same time—and launch a rocket at the other side. When I warned him against such acts, he jokingly accused me of not having enough courage.

Maslakh/Karantina Under Siege, First Massacre of the Civil War

One evening, I was asked as well as 19 other young volunteer recruits to be ready to go to battle. I reported to base. We all prepared ourselves . . . AK-

47s, hand grenades, many cartridges filled with bullets . . . No one briefed us about where we were going or what our mission was. Shortly afterward, we were loaded in civilian cars, four in each, plus the driver. It was about 2 A.M. The cars took off driving in a caravan. I asked where our destination was, and the driver responded, "Maslakh." I had never been there in my life. It was a slum neighborhood, also known as Karantina, a sheep trading area with slaughterhouses, which is how it got its name. *Maslakh,* in Arabic, means "a slaughterhouse." It was located on the western foothill of Ashrafieh, a Christian hilltop suburb of East Beirut known to host leadership offices and a stronghold base of Kataeb. Some of their leaders resided in the prestigious quarters of the suburb.

In the car with me were a couple of guys I knew. In the other cars were Fakhri, my childhood friend, and Fathi, a younger kid, son of a neighbor, who lived in the same building as I did in Sabra. I cared about him like a relative. Amer was in another car, and Hassan, a childhood classmate was in another. Driving from West to East Beirut during battles was stupid enough; driving in a caravan of five cars following each other closely must have been the epitome of stupidity. These were the only five cars on the road at that time, and in wartime, no less. I was 18 years old at the time. I was sitting in the backseat on the left side, behind the driver. While the caravan cars were traveling alongside the southern foothills of Ashrafieh, bullets with nighttime markers were fired at us. They flew over our cars. Since I saw the location of the shooter, and against strict instructions not to fire, I could not restrain myself. I lowered myself in my seat, aimed my Kalashnikov, and started shooting toward the assailants. The men in the other cars in front and behind me, followed suit. Suddenly, all the windows in the five cars were lit up shooting in defense.

Our drivers drove much faster than their normal, supposed-to-be-camouflaged ride. It took us a few minutes to get under a bridge. It was dark. We got out of the cars, and suddenly, all hell broke loose. Heavy gun shelling and heavy machine guns were being fired. The drivers got mad at me for starting the whole firing back ordeal. I did not regret it, though. I just did not want to be a sitting duck until a bullet hit me or any of my friends.

We were able to travel far into East Beirut at that time. There was no checkpoint to stop our cars. There could've been one, and we all might have been butchered. To this day I wonder why the road from the west side to our destination Maslakh had no Kataeb or other Christian right-wing checkpoints. From under the bridge, Maslakh was only a short run away. The car drivers turned back, headed to the West side, and I never heard if they all made it back. All 20 of us made it into Maslakh, running one at a time, with about 100 feet between each. Bullets were flying all over the place, but none of us got hit.

We reached a three-story concrete building inside the slum neighborhood. It was an unfinished construction of a future school. The ground floor was a base. At least 50 fighters were stationed there, slept there, ate there, and went to the front lines to fight. We just sat on the floor to rest. I was then thinking of how that whole thing did not make sense to me . . . How I was used like a robot, not knowing anything and just ending up in an islandlike situation . . . with no way to go back unless I wanted to get killed on the road, or in a neighborhood which seems to be at the bottom of a hilltop where enemy forces were dug in their castlelike front. I questioned myself, what were we doing there?

I could not sleep that early morning until I was completely exhausted. I slept only a couple of hours, woke up, and started learning about the place by talking to other fighters, not from any leader. I found out Maslakh had only a handful of Palestinian families and a good number of Lebanese of Bedouin tribes who raised and sold sheep. We had no strong following amongst them, and we could hardly trust anyone there. There was no leader of our group of 20. Every four had a leader, and I was a leader of four. Hassan was a leader of four, Fakhri was a leader, and Amer was a leader. Hassan decided he did not want to be a leader. He just went off and stationed himself with one other guy at the front lines. His guys were abandoned, so they joined me.

In the morning, the area military leader whose name was Qais came over. He stood there and demanded, "I need a few guys to go with me." Fakhri and Fathi and two others went with him. They both came back shot. Fakhri was hit in his upper leg, Fathi in his abdomen. We got them in a Red Cross ambulance and said our good-byes before they were transported to West Beirut. By then, ambulances were allowed to go back and forth. The two other guys of Fakhri's group joined me. It was shortly after that all the guys who came in the caravan recognized we all needed to band together as a group. We did not have much confidence in the way things were being run by Qais.

The next day, he came over again and wanted to send five of our guys to the front. I confronted him and said, "No, you are not taking any of our group. You need to assign a location where we are all together responsible to defend and leave us alone."

He said, "This is mutiny."

I said, "You can call it whatever you want, but this is the way it is."

He left and did not come back. We took upon ourselves to guard front lines closer to our base. Every hour passing in Maslakh made me more aware of how weak our defenses were. We had no heavy guns or machine guns, and not enough men to put up a long fight, given that we were facing a monstrous area, a place where Kataeb had some of their best fighting units. I was worried that we all would end up slaughtered in what is called the slaughterhouse. Only a few guys were guarding each street. I made calls to our leaders in West Beirut and told them on the phone, that we were in desperate need of weapons and fighters. Otherwise, the place would not last long. I was shocked about the conditions of the place, and further shocked about how no serious efforts were being shown to support us there.

More anxiety occurred when a local guy who claimed to have gone into Ashrafieh told our fighters that he saw Kataeb forces, along with the Maghaweer, the Lebanese army special forces known for being the most skillful and ruthless fighters, gathered across from us, getting ready to storm the place. The guy kept telling stories in a way which made me suspect he was a spy on a mission for the other side. I observed him for a couple of days. He would come every day, clean shaved, freshly clothed, and spread fear and more rumors. Finally, I had him arrested, took his weapon away, and I personally interrogated him. I was surrounded by two big men in my group. The guy was quick to give it all away. He told me he was spying on us. He drew maps of the streets and how many guys were guarding each street, and what kind of weapons they carried. He knew the routes we were getting our food supplies. Hearing all that made me feel betrayed by this guy, really scared. If our enemy knew all that information, we all were as good as dead.

I went back and shared what I learned with whoever mattered. We fortified all streets which we thought were most likely to be attacked, made a lot of false movements all over Maslakh, just to put up a show that we had fighters all over the place, moved our weapons around, and the one shelling gun we had, we moved it around from place to place to pretend we had a number of shelling guns. Whether that worked or not, I had no idea. We kept the spy jailed. At one point, our leadership in West Beirut sent a senior officer who sneaked in to meet with us and listen to our needs. I met him, gave him a list of essential needs, including a list of weapons, ammunition, and more men. He promised the leadership would act on it. When I told him about the spy and asked what we should do with him, the officer said, "Take him out in an open area and have him executed."

I said, "Just like that?"

He said, "Yes."

I could not do that. I could not have someone executed. The idea was totally insane. I could not live with such an action, even though the guy confessed to me about everything he did. I doubted my skills because I thought to myself, *I am not a professional interrogator, and God will never forgive me for causing the death of someone in captivity.* I thought that was not something God can forgive. I did not act upon or even tell anyone what the officer said. I just kept him captive, and I thought I would later turn him over to security people who could find out more about the guy. However, the spy made me mistrust all the residents of that place except the group that came with me from Sabra.

We remained vigilant, extra careful, and worried any moment that an all-out attack was to come and finish us off. Maslakh had no chance to push back any serious attack. No weapons and no ammunition arrived while I was there, or after, for that matter. A shaky cease-fire was announced, and before it was broken again, a group of another 20 young men arrived to replace us. They also came from Sabra, led by my good friend Nidal. I met him upon arrival. I said, "What the hell are you doing here? It's only a matter of time before this place will be stormed by the Kataeb and taken over. The leadership is not serious about defending it. It's a stupid thing altogether."

Nidal just shook his head and told me not to worry. He and the others would be OK, and he said that more help was on the way. I, along with my group, got into the cars which brought Nidal and his group, and headed back to Sabra. The spy was taken to security headquarters for further questioning. I never found out what happened to him.

When we arrived, we were greeted like those who came back from the dead. I went straight to check on Fathi, this young blue-eyed, blond guy who looked up to me like I was his older brother. When he saw me while lying in his hospital bed, he cried and hugged me in disbelief that I was actually standing right there. He did not think I would come out alive. Fathi recovered from his wound and was lucky to survive it with no permanent damage; the same with Fakhri, who was in better shape. He was limping for a while, though. He was lucky the shot only tore through his thigh muscles. No nerves or bones were damaged.

Our families and friends heard about the siege of Maslakh on the news almost daily. People knew we were under siege, and it was only a matter of time for us before we met our fate. Thank God that did not happen to my group, and it did not happen to Nidal's group either, but it happened a few months later, on January 18, 1976.

On January 18, Maslakh was attacked by a coalition of the Christian right-wing militia forces. An estimated 1,500 people were massacred in the place. Whoever got out alive was chased out in fear toward West Beirut. It became known as the Maslakh/Karantina Massacre, and it marked the first of many ethnic-cleansing massacres which took place during the Lebanese civil war of 1975.

A month before, in an area attached to downtown Beirut on a Saturday, people were going about their lives and the cease-fire was in effect. Kataeb gunmen went on a wild killing spree, setting up checkpoints, checking civilian passersby, checking their IDs. A Palestinian was killed in an ugly way, and a Muslim Lebanese was either killed or kidnapped. Gunmen spread out into downtown Beirut as far as they could, killing numerous people or kidnapping them. That day became known as Black Saturday.

Justifications and explanations were announced by the Kataeb and Christian right-wing leaders for this behavior. It was claimed that those who committed the acts were unruly members avenging the death of four of their comrades found killed earlier in East Beirut. That incident should have indicated what Kataeb and other Christian right-wing factions were capable of. In one month's time, the civil war was taken to a whole different level—that of mass killings and religious ethnic cleansing, which unraveled and escalated.

The Town of Damour

Only two days after the Maslakh/Karantina Massacre, Palestinian and Lebanese coalition forces attacked the southern coastal town of Damour, controlled by Christian right-wing forces. It was located a few kilometers south of Beirut, in a critical location which could delay movement of troops and supplies of both Palestinian and Lebanese National Movement fighters to and from Beirut where the headquarters were located. The revenge rampage was unleashed, the talk in West Beirut was that Kataeb and their allies must learn a hard lesson after the massacre they committed. Damour then had to pay the price.

The town was attacked from the north, northeast, south, and southeast. In later years, I happen to meet the Palestinian commander known as Abu Saleh, in Damascus, in the mid-eighties. He told me and a friend of mine a part of the Damour story, when he commanded the forces attacking from the north and northeast. While Commander Abu Musa led forces from the south and southeast, Abu Saleh talked to Abu Musa via wireless communication and told him, "Let's both press on with the attack late evening. I will meet you for breakfast in the center of Damour." They met their goal, Damour fell by morning hours, despite a reputation of having some of the toughest fighters. They were no match for the Palestinian commanders experienced in fighting the much-tougher Israeli army. Civilians were killed in Damour, residents of the town fled, nuns and priests were hiding in the town church until they were escorted out by Palestinians sent by Arafat himself.

The town was looted by paramilitary and militia men who came in after the town fell and the professional fighters withdrew. Elderly men and women were left behind, scared and hungry. They were put on buses and trucks, transported to a girls' school which was on summer break in Sabra, out of all places. I was asked along with a couple of friends, about three of us, to make sure Damour refugees were protected and taken care of during their stay. I met these people. I remember they seemed scared at first, disoriented. They never spoke of the horrors they experienced during the battle of Damour. Neither did my friends nor I ask them about it. Days later, they seemed less scared but still very cautious and uncertain of what could happen to them. We just made sure they were guarded, fed, had a place to sleep, a cover, and a bath. A few weeks later, they were transported to East Beirut. The people of Damour were ethnically cleansed as well. Their town where they and their grandfathers lived was mostly destroyed and became empty for a good number of years.

Change of Tides

In the early part of 1976, battles seemed to be going in favor of the PLO and its Lebanese National Movement allies. Many areas were taken over by battle, including downtown Beirut, the famous Beirut Hotel Quarter along the beach, and the commercial markets of downtown Beirut. Forces were also pushing from the east to the west in the high mountains typically held by Christian right-wing forces. All seemed to be going well for the PLO and its Lebanese allies. A new political map to include a new regime structure in Lebanon was being discussed in intellectual circles and between national movement parties . . . a regime with no religious divisions, a new democracy, and, of course, progressive and supportive of the PLO. Kataeb and their allies were being routed out; their spirits were very low, while we in West Beirut and all other areas expected victory to arrive in a few weeks.

When I was bored very late at night or in the early-morning hours, while at the base in Sabra, battles were still raging at many hot spots between the Christian right enclave, as it became known then, and the surrounding areas, and I would either receive a phone call, or I would make one to the Kataeb office in Ashrafieh. During the first call or two, we exchanged insults, called each other sons of whores and the like, then we calmed down and just discussed our opposing points of view. The Kataeb guy and I would talk for an hour and a half. It was during a time they were facing many defeats. I would tell him they were finished, that I was going to personally meet him soon . . . if he was still alive . . . when we got to his neighborhood. He said they were determined to fight to the end. I tried to understand why they hated the Palestinians so much when all we wanted was to go home to Palestine. He said that Palestinians are liars; they just want to occupy Lebanon with their allies and make it their home. When either one of us got tired and wanted to end the conversation, one of us would tease the other by saying something like, "You better go hide in a basement now, because I am off to launch a few missiles your way."

During these days, another truce was declared, and a calm took place for a while.

My father was never impressed by the Palestinian revolution, especially its leadership. Neither Arafat nor other leaders were up to the mission, he believed. My father suffered from emphysema for many years. I watched him suffer in silence. He would be sitting in a chair on the balcony of our apartment with a transistor battery-operated radio as it was known at the time. I would be coming home or just passing by next to the building. I would look up, make eye contact and wave at him, and he would wave back and smile. At that age, I got to know my father a lot more than previously. We would have our Turkish coffee time together on the balcony, talk about almost everything . . . sometimes politics, and other times he would pass on words of wisdom which I would always remember as I grew older. It was during these conversations that I learned of my father's times of both pride and regrets. Even during his sickness and financial difficulties, my father was a proud man.

That was a time during which I put my parents through some rather sleepless nights—like when I took off with the fighters, and all they knew was that I was out there somewhere in the middle of hell which broke loose all over Beirut. I can imagine how they felt when I was out there, and all they heard was machine-gun fire and explosions of heavy gun shells. I used to show up at home early in the morning, and they would receive me with such relief that I was still alive and in one piece.

It was that year that my father fell into one of his weaker cycles. He wanted to rest and sleep, but he was in a lot pain although he did not complain. I thought, just like before, it was a passing episode; however, his condition got worse. One afternoon I went and brought a doctor from an adjacent neighborhood. I just walked around asking where I could find a doctor, which was the norm for people like us. The doctor walked with me to our home. He examined my father and gave him a shot. Only God knows what was in that shot. I was too young and too ignorant to know. I don't know if he even explained my father's condition to anyone, including my mother. That would have been the common practice at that time. Most doctors felt like they were dealing with ignorant people. Their attitude was that even if they tried to explain, we would not understand anyway, so they just went about doing their job. They gave quick and very abbreviated answers and finished by saying that hopefully the patient will get better. The only difference in this case, I heard him tell someone near me that my father won't get better. He did not say my father needed hospitalization. He just left it at that. I paid him his fees, and he departed.

A few hours later my father's condition deteriorated severely. I was in our sitting room when I heard loud prayers spoken by my grandmother, my aunt, and my mother. I jumped up and went into my father's bedroom. The women were surrounding him and reciting versus of the Quran loudly. I freaked out and screamed at them to step away from him, to give him space. I talked to him.

"Yaba," I said, which is Arabic for "Dad."

He answered, "Yaba," which meant ("Yes, son," in colloquial Arabic). That was the last word I heard from my father. My thoughts were racing. I thought my father always lacked oxygen. I thought if only I gave him oxygen he would be OK. I remembered there was a hospital treating the war casualties right across the street from us, so I ran out of the apartment, ran down the stairs, ran across the street right into the hospital emergency room, screaming, "Give me oxygen, I need oxygen!" The nurses and hospital staff looked at me with such bewilderment. They did not know what to think as I reached for a big oxygen container and wanted to just carry to my father. Finally, someone asked me what I needed it for. I told him my father needed oxygen. Two men grabbed a patient stretcher and told me to take them to him. "We will bring him here."

I ran, and they ran behind me. When we arrived home, they put my father on the stretcher, and I assisted in carrying him with them. We took him down the stairs and back to the hospital. As the doctor was checking him, he politely asked me to wait outside of the room seeing my condition and possibly fearing my reaction. I guess the doctor did not want to give me the bad news. He let one of the male nurses do it.

The man approached me and said, "I'm sorry, your father passed away."

At my side was Abu Nayif, a man older than my father and a good neighbor. He held my arm gently and asked me to pray for my father. I was so defiant and so angry at God. I just looked up at the sky and yelled, "Why did you do that?! Why did you take

152

his life?" I blamed God because I had learned even as a young child that God gives life, and God takes away life.

The walk back to our home felt like the longest walk I had to take in my life even though it was right across the street and two stories up in the building. By then, our home was filled with neighbors, women, then men came, and relatives started arriving . . . all crying and wailing while I was still in total shock of what happened. I withdrew from everyone to a quiet corner and just hoped that was a bad nightmare which would go away. But it did not.

It rained that night, the first time for the season. The next morning it started to feel like a new reality. I went to the room where, by then, my father's body was lying in his bed, and I talked to him in a reproachful voice. "Why did you have to leave?" I truly felt a catastrophic loss in my life, one of great emotional magnitude. My uncles and relatives took me to the living room, where the men were sitting to show support. My uncle knew I was a smoker in secret, as it was considered disrespectful to smoke against the will of the parents. He pulled out his pack of cigarettes and offered me one. It was an indirect reminder that I was a man now, and I needed to get my act together. I took the cigarette and smoked it.

The next day was the funeral, as it is customary in Islam and dignified to hold funerals as soon as possible after the passing of someone. I was in a terrible shape, consumed by sadness, and not having slept the night took a toll on me. The cemetery was within a relatively short walking distance from the apartment building. Muhannad, my close friend, appeared and walked by my side. We went into the mosque, prayed for my father, continued on to the cemetery, completed the funeral proceedings, and returned home, where more and more people including old friends of my father came to show their respect and offer condolences. It went on for a week, then slowed down after that. My father's absence was a rude awakening for me, and a close encounter for me as an adult through the death of the man God chose to be my father . . . The person who shaped a good part of me and will always influence my life. Most of the time whenever I approached the apartment building or passed it on my way to somewhere else, I always looked up to the balcony and waved my hand in one motion, just to remember my father who was no longer there.

My father's life captivated me . . . His success, marriage, loss of fortune, sickness, good heart, pride, and wisdom deeply affected me. Ever since my childhood I had hoped my father's health would improve, that someday he was going be strong again and improve his life condition and, therefore, his family's.

I spent a lot of time in my mind analyzing my father's life, what he did and how things turned out. What could have been done differently? My siblings' childhood as well as mine was not an easy one, especially due to my father's siblings and his parents being way too close for comfort . . . too much interference in our lives . . . many of them considered themselves authority figures to rule our lives. Despite my mother's constant complaints, my father did not or could not make a change. His financial means and his inability to separate from his parents' nuclear household and his own nuclear household caused much psychological stress to all of his children. By the time he began to recognize it, the damage had already occurred. We had a family model that was filled with confusion and dysfunction, which we all had to live with all of our lives. It is not simple to change established childhood patterns, even after one acknowledges them and tries to replace them. They still creep up in the mind and affect our lives at a subconscious level. These experiences did not just scar our minds and hearts, they also deeply affected our behavior, our close relationships. In my case, the affect was obvious in my marriage, my overprotection of my kids, my fear of a sickness like my father's, and my fear of financial loss. In other words, I feared becoming the weak version of my father.

During those days, Beirut was a very sad and rundown city. Many buildings and roads were in ruins; neighborhoods were ruled by men with guns on the streets. Shelling from both sides and explosions in civilian-populated areas sometimes caused a great loss of life. I witnessed this happening a few times, sometimes just a block away from our apartment or office. Muhannad used to visit me regularly. He showed up on our doorstep one day shaken since a gun shell landed a few yards away from where he was walking in an open area near our home. He was lucky that day.

Fakhri, my childhood friend, was offered a trip to Moscow for a year to join a youth program. Jareer took off for university studies in England. Nidal lived in a neighborhood of Shayah. During the relatively quiet days of the truce, he was among his troop, well admired and looked up to. He had a habit of quick engagements to pretty girls. Knowing Nidal, I never thought he was serious about getting married to any of his many fiancées. I thought that it was his way to legitimize a relationship with a girl so they both could be much more comfortable amongst friends and the local community.

One day the truce broke down, so gunmen on both sides ran like mad setting up fortified positions on the street sides. Cars whizzed by fast, blowing their horns. Peddlers on the streets picked up their goods and retreated to safety. People walked fast or ran to their homes to be with their loved ones. Washed clothes which hung on ropes on balconies to dry were being picked up and taken inside, then windows and balcony doors were closed. Panic reigned everywhere. This always preceded the start of battles between neighborhoods, and cross fire between buildings of East and West Beirut.

Nidal, along with a couple of his comrades in arms, set up midsized automatic guns on Asaad Al Asaad , one of the most famous streets of Shayah, known for being dangerously wide to cross and very close to the opposite side. Nidal so busy with the task at hand that he totally ignored a Lebanese army tank across the intersection. He partly ignored it because some Lebanese army units were stationed on such contentious intersections with the official mission of separating the warring parties and keeping the peace. Nidal did not know keeping peace was also interpreted by some Lebanese army commanders sympathetic to the other side as forcing peace . . . and that was done by quelling—or even firing at— anyone with a gun. The tank aimed at Nidal's position and fired a shell straight at him, hitting the sandbags in front of him and blowing Nidal's arm away while filling his face and chest with shrapnel. Nidal was picked up by his comrades, put in a car, and raced off to the Sabra hospital across from my home. That day, the emergency room received a few wounded men. I was home at the time and did not notice my comrades. Although the men were quick to bring Nidal to the hospital, one look at his wounds by one of the emergency doctors was enough to know the doctor was not able to handle the case. He told the guys to take him to the Makasid hospital a mile away, surrounded by crowded concrete buildings and narrow streets of the neighborhood. And so they took Nidal there.

At the emergency room of Makasid hospital, the doctor examined Nidal with wounds in his chest near his heart, his blown-off arm, and cuts all over his face, and quickly told them, "He's done. There's no way to save him." His friends were very hot

158

tempered. They held the doctor at gunpoint, told him to take Nidal into the operating room, and save him or die. The doctor obeyed. Nidal was in surgery for many hours, and then was sent to the intensive care unit.

By then I was aware of his situation and arrived. Nidal looked like he had been butchered. Only about 6 inches of his left arm remained. He also lost his left eye. His face was filled with stitches and bandaged, and his chest was stitched up and covered with bandages as well. He had wires and tubes coming out of him which connected to monitoring machines. I thought Nidal would not survive that. The guys showed me a partly burnt hat he was wearing. It was my hat, a Russian-style hat, and Nidal wanted it so much that I could not turn him down and gave it to him, even though it was a present from my sister Samira.

A couple of days later, Nidal was suddenly moved to what is known as third-degree care of the hospital, a place where nurses' and doctors' care was known to be substandard. While it was sufficient for lightly injured people, it was the worst place in the hospital for Nidal. I was contacted and informed of the move. Many of our friends tried to influence the hospital to make other arrangements. I personally headed to Arafat's office, just walked in, and said, "I want to meet Arafat." People in his office looked at me strangely. After verifying that I was one of them they asked me to wait. I did, and soon, into the room walked the well-known Ali Hassan Salameh ("Abu Hassan"). He was Arafat's security chief. It was my first time meeting him. He was indeed a charismatic man in addition to being tall and handsome. He later married the former Miss Universe, the Lebanese Georgina Rizk.

Abu Hassan asked me what brought me to Arafat's office. I told him I needed his help to move Nidal to a better care level at the hospital; otherwise, we were about to lose a great freedom fighter named Nidal. He listened politely, pulled a cigarette, lit it, took a puff, pulled a sheet of paper with Arafat's office logo on it, and wrote a letter to the hospital director to make the move. I thanked him, took the letter, and ran to Makasid. I found out Nidal had already been moved into first-degree care. I did not know or ask how or who did it. I was just glad for Nidal's sake.

Nidal did survive, and he got an artificial left arm and left eye. He improved, but he was never the same. At first everyone around us showed him much love and support. Nidal moved to live in a little room at the base, but he was weak and fragile. Muhannad and I did our best to keep him company and boost his morale. He became stronger physically; however, his behavior was that of a defeated and depressed person. That confident, charming, handsome, and funny Nidal was, by then, gone forever; He became sarcastic and showed underlying bitterness. He tried to joke and be funny. He even sang and made fun of his missing arm. His friends went along with him, but the feeling we felt inside was very sad.

At times, Nidal would be mean toward his friends. Being close to him, I took a good share of this behavior. Eventually, he moved to live with friends in a nearby neighborhood. One evening, Nidal was out and came to the base looking for me. I heard his loud voice, and I could tell he was totally drunk. I did not want him to get close to where some guys and I were hanging out. I did not want them to see him in such a condition. That would undermine their respect for him, so I walked up to him and asked him to take a walk with me. He cried and told me he was thinking of killing himself. He had a Magnum .45 pistol attached to his side by his belt as was usual for him. However, that was the first time I thought to myself he could just use it to kill himself. I felt he was reaching out to me. We walked and talked for hours. I told him that he was still the same person and none of our friends felt any different, and that was a true statement. Somehow, we all interacted with Nidal the same way we did before. It seemed to me his wounds were much deeper and more hurtful inside than what showed on his body.

Our original group was down to Nidal and I, especially after Muhannad left for the U.S. to pursue his undergraduate degree. By then, Jareer was already in England for the same reason. Fakhri still in Moscow, Amer in the Emirates, and Abu Bakr was in one of the Arab oil-producing countries. I never saw Abu Bakr again since that time.

Syrian Intervention

The Israeli and other support of the Christian right-wing alliance was not strong enough to make a big difference on the ground. Only a strong ground force intervention stronger than all the warring factions would change the war results that came from Syria, and it was opposite to expectations and in favor of the Kataeb and their allies. Somehow, the PLO leadership was getting closer to President Anwar Sadat, of Egypt, who led his country during the 1973 war, and thereafter, he was looking to make peace with Israel. He was maneuvering on his own and left the late president Assad of Syria out of the game. Most likely, it was due to Assad's less-compromising beliefs and his nontrusting approach of Israel and the U.S as well.

The Palestinian factor, as has been the case historically, was vital for any peace process. When the PLO chose the Sadat track, it created a wedge between itself and the Syrian regime of Hafez al-Assad. Relations changed from alliance to animosity, which continued through the later years until the death of both leaders. The late President Assad seemed to have directly or indirectly convinced the U.S. and Israel not to intervene while he received a mandate from the Arab League to lead a multi-Arab military force, which was to be deployed in Lebanon, to separate the warring parties and restore peace and order to Lebanon.

The Syrians pushed into Lebanon with an obvious agenda of weakening the PLO, and given one of the PLO factions, Al-Saeqa (the Lightning Force), was part of the Syrian Baath organization, the Syrian influence went a long way in trying to position

Syria as the main player in any potential peace process negotiations, one which would have granted Syria a regional leading role. The Syrian forces fought and crushed any resistance on their way from the eastern mountains toward Beirut. Palestinian fighters and their Lebanese allies could not stand in their way for long. The Syrian army was gigantic in comparison. They did, however, put up a good fight to slow the army's advance, especially in the town of Bhamdoun overlooking Beirut. In a battle of only a few hours inside the main square of Sidon, a city located 20 kilometers south of Beirut, Fatah fighters destroyed 18 Syrian Soviet-made tanks. Fatah commander Abu Musa led that battle. The next morning, Lebanese newspapers showed pictures of the destroyed tanks. The biggest highlight was one tank's tower and its heavy gun which was hit by a Palestinian rocket and had flown and landed on top of a building overlooking the street. It was a humiliating battle for the Syrian army. One condition of the cease-fire declared a couple of days later was to remove that tank from that rooftop. It was too late for the PLO to change the course of events. Syrian "containment," as the Syrian objective was labeled by Fatah, was coming, and it was only a matter of how to minimize it and counter it through pressure of other Arab PLO allies.

While this was taking place in the mountains and outside major cities of Lebanon, Fatah and its supporting Palestinian factions decided to get rid of what was considered a Syrian Trojan horse, "Al-Saeqa," and its ally, the "PFLP General Command," a splinter group of the Popular Front for the Liberation of Palestine. The battle began one evening when we were assembled at the base. Nidal, having recovered from his injuries, and I were selected to lead a group to occupy Saeqa offices located close to our base in a six-story building. We were informed the building was already empty of any Saeqa fighters or activists, who seemed to have fled the scene in a rush to avoid a battle which would have been fierce. But most likely, they would have been defeated. Resentment toward them was powerful in all Palestinian camps and neighborhoods of Lebanon.

Nidal and I, followed by at least 10 other fighters, approached the building, walking slowly and cautiously as would fighters on hostile ground do. We got to the entrance, where we met no resistance, then we walked up the stairs. Someone was coming down. Nidal put the gun to his chest. The guy was so scared and was quick to say, "I just live here. The fighters are gone," and so we let him go and continued up the stairs, very worried, and rightfully so. It would only take one fighter to throw a hand grenade toward us, which would have killed us in a flash. Luckily, that never happened. No fighters were there. We broke into their offices and weapons storage rooms. It was obvious they left in a hurry, and left all kinds of weapons behind. I was shocked to see a tennis ball-like object, which I have never seen before right in the middle of the weapons storage room. Nidal was quick to warn me not to touch it, for it explodes with the wrong touch. It was placed there on purpose for us to fall into a trap. We would have been vaporized when it exploded, which would have triggered the whole weapons room to explode. We secured the place and went back.

Walking back, we passed many men who had already received word the place was secured and under control. They came to confiscate the weapons and transport them to our base.

The next morning, we were at another Saeqa location, except that one was much more important. It was the headquarters of the late Zuhair Mohsin, the leader of the pro-Syrian faction. Close to his office were a few other offices and huge weapons storage located belowground of an eight-story residential building. Saeqa fighters at their security offices and close to the residence of their leader put up a fight for a day and withdrew heading east. Kataeb and other Lebanese Christian right-wing forces offered them safe passage to the mountains where Syrian forces were stationed.

Learning of the Saeqa fighters' flight, civilians and fighters of other factions rushed to the evacuated offices to loot them. I will never forget when some other fighters and I went down to the underground weapons storage. We witnessed civilians and some fighters as well carrying boxes of ammunition, guns, boxes filled with explosive materials, and whatever else they could put their hands on, which would later be sold for a tidy profit. Some of them were stepping on rockets, 107 millimeter rockets, and explosive objects that were all over the place. It was a miracle that day a terrible disaster did not happen. An explosion would have killed everyone in that storage area, and I am sure it would have brought down the whole eight-story residential building as well, killing hundreds of people who lived there. God works in mysterious ways to protect the ignorant, even if sometimes greedy.

After the chasing out of pro-Syrian Palestinian factions, a new alliance was formed between the fleeing factions and the Kataeb and Christian right-wing, along with the Syrian army forces, an alliance which came to cause a major defeat to the Palestinians in the battle and tragedy of Tal Zaatar.

Tal Zaatar (Hill of Thyme)

During that time, Tal Zaatar, a Palestinian refugee camp, housed close to 60,000 people. It was located in East Beirut, farther east of Maslakh/Karantina, totally disconnected from Palestinians or their supporters in Lebanon. It was completely surrounded by Kataeb and their allies and supporters. The camp had been surrounded and was placed under a long siege. It was sealed off. No one could get in or out. They killed any Palestinian they could lay their eyes on. No food, medicine, or water was allowed in. For over 6 months, vicious battles took place around the camp, with heavy guns shelling the camp in the thousands every day. Kataeb military force founder and chief William Hawi was shot and killed by Palestinian fighters while leading battles against the camp. Death became a regular companion of the people in Tal Zaatar. The injured died either of bleeding out or infections caused by wounds. Everyone accepted the death of a brother, sister, mother, father, or a friend as a normal event, since they believed they, too, were about to meet the same fate. No cease-fire agreement was kept; no serious negotiations took place about the fate of the camp and its residents; and battles and shelling continued while the whole world watched. Any diplomatic effort fell far short of what was needed to stop the bloodshed and end the siege.

News from the camp via wireless communication told of the horrors and terrible conditions people of the camp were enduring. The PLO was trying to put pressure on other fronts to ease the intensity of the firepower and attacks on the camp. The Syrian army, some Lebanese army units, and the Saeqa faction were all helping Kataeb and their allies against the refugee camp. Bachir Gemayel, son of Pierre Gemayel, the founder of Kataeb, was appointed military chief of Kataeb. He was well-known for his extreme hatred of Palestinians, Syrians, and Arabs, in general, while he was fond of the Zionist leaders. Bachir vowed to erase Tal Zaatar off the face of the earth.

Food and medicine became scarce. Palestinian forces and their allies pooled their forces and tried to attack from Shayah. The goal was to take over the main roads leading to Tal Zaatar. I was called to participate along with many others. I was with Palestinian professional soldiers who were part of the PLO regular army units. Our mission was to open fire on the northern side of Ain al-Rummaneh with enough intensity that would convince the opposite side that a penetration attempt will take place from that spot. Meanwhile, a much-larger Palestinian force was to attack from the south side and occupy the roads leading to the camp under siege. We did our part, with intense fire, rocket-propelled grenades, artillery shells, then individual soldiers firing, until the early-morning hours.

When light broke out, I took a break, along with a friend, and headed south to learn about the anticipated good news of our forces penetrating east. There was no good news. The attack was called off. No one knew what the reason was. In later weeks, we knew the reason was an ultimatum issued by the Syrian regime to the PLO to call off the attack or face a Syrian attack which would liquidate the PLO presence in Beirut. I never understood why Syria supported the annihilation of that camp. Maybe it was a show of goodwill, and a favor in advance for a payback down the road when Syrian forces needed to consolidate their presence in Lebanon. Shortly after the failure of a full-fledge attack, the PLO leadership resorted to other simple

170

and less-effective methods, like trying to sneak fighters into Tal Zaatar from the mountains.

Monte Verde

One day I was called to lead a group of four. We were transported to a mountain town called Abadiyeh. A hundred or so fighters were gathered at a mountain ridge. Down below was a deep valley, and across was the small Christian village called Monte Verde (Green Mount). Our mission was to occupy it with a shock attack and turn it into a base, from where fighters could infiltrate around the nearby town of Mansouriyeh and on into Tal Zaatar. Theoretically, that sounded logical; realistically, it was another crazy idea. Monte Verde is located a stone's throw away from Beit Mary, which was another stronghold of Kataeb and its allies. Of course, as fighters, we got to know that much later . . . only when we were on the outer edge of Monte Verde. When we started our march downhill toward the valley below, it was around 8 or 9 in the evening.

From the mountaintops of Beit Mary, Kataeb forces were firing direct artillery shells at our side. We walked in a long line of over 100 fighters as if these shells and heavy machine-gun fire was not even there. We kept on walking. It was early morning when we arrived at the bottom of the hill. Fearing to be seen by the enemy from the opposite mountain above and having been exhausted by the mountain walk down the hill all night, we disbursed ourselves under trees and slept, while we took turns guarding the sleeping fighters. We woke up, whispered to each other if we wanted to talk, opened some cans of food, and ate. Around 6 in the evening, we started heading up the opposite hill toward Monte Verde. Going up that hill was one of the worst hikes I ever made during peace or war. We had a guide, but he must have been guessing that section of the trip. I had to use my AK-47 as a cane to stick in the ground when we encountered a gravel area uphill. Some of us slid down. Luckily, no one slid enough to take a couple of other fighters with him so that we would all go rolling down the mount we were climbing up.

It was around 3 in the morning when we got to the first mountaintop. It was dark. We could hear pigs and others noises. We then discovered we were very close to a small pig farm. We took a rest for only a half hour, then a commander called each group of fighters at a time and guided them to different location points, spreading out the 100 or so fighters in the area. My group of five, including myself, was stationed under a hilltop in some grove with fruit trees. I looked up the hill and did not like it. We were too close and too vulnerable. We could be seen from above. I said to the commander, "This is not a good place." He brushed me off, and with an attitude like "what do you know?" told us to stay there, and left, That's it. We had no idea where the other fighters were. If fighters approached us, we wouldn't know if they were friends or foes. We did not even have any communication device like wireless walkie-talkies or any other transmitter. We kept quiet and just stayed under trees awaiting further orders of what to do next.

A few hours later, a farmer riding a donkey came into the grove. He greeted us. We talked. He knew we were Palestinians. He was a Druze Lebanese. We had no idea the area had some Druze as well. He was friendly, as expected. After all, what else can a farmer do when he walks into his grove and finds five fighters stationed there and ready for battle? The farmer stayed and worked until around 3 in the afternoon. We still had no instructions of what to do. I thought we should at least hold the farmer and his relative who came around noon. We did not, however. We let them both go.

About an hour later, shooting from the hills above started and bullets whistled above our heads. We could not even know where exactly the gunfire was coming from, except it was from a distance. Shortly afterward, heavy machine guns sounded, and artillery shells were falling in our area. I left my group and went to check with some leader about what to do. I did not see a leader, however, just saw some fighters retreating downhill. I asked one of them what we were supposed to do. One yelled back to me, "Everyone is on his own now, so find your way." I ran back, called my group members, and we all headed down the hill again. Soon, darkness fell, so I felt better, but not for long as the Kataeb shot artillery shells to lighten the sky and the ground below.

One of my group members was a man named Adnan, a dark short fellow with a heavy body and who was quiet most of the time. I asked how long he had been a fighter. He answered, "A week." He could hardly use an AK-47, let alone maneuver his way in a battlefield. I asked him, "What the hell are you doing with us?" He said his family was in Tal Zaatar, and he wanted to get there to protect them.

While retreating slowly, I saw another group leader who advised me not to head back the same way we came, as it was wide open and exposed to enemy fire. We could be easy targets. So we decided once we were in the valley again to just walk north, then start climbing back from a different location. By then, there were no longer 100 fighters anymore. There was only a maximum group of 5 to 10 at a time, disbursed in the valley. We would hear noise from trees, so we would point a gun up and ask, "Who's there?" Another fighter would reply, "One of you." Eventually a few fighters would reunite with us, and our group became about 25 to 30. We walked quietly. Some told us of other fighters who died on the way bleeding from injuries. A few went back the same way and were shot. Others told of an incident where three Kataeb fighters in a Jeep with a heavy machine gun sped down the hill. Not knowing how far in their area we were, they found themselves in the middle of our fighters. Marwan, a comrade, targeted it with a rocket-propelled grenade. They also shot him in the foot. He was lucky to be able to limp his way with not much bleeding, and made it back safely.

Eventually, we stopped and slept under trees. In the morning, we started heading up the hill to the east mountain where we thought our forces might be. It was a quiet day, hardly any machine-gun fire, no artillery. The area uphill was a forest; great cover for us. We continued our climb but were lost. One fighter had a transmitter, but he could not dare use it for fear of getting discovered.

We saw a water pipe, like a 24-inch pipe. We decided this must lead us to a town somewhere, so we followed the pipe north. At one point, the pipe was extended from the hill we were on, hanging in the air going to another hill across with a deep valley below. That was a disappointment. We decided to just walk up the hill we were on. After an hour's climb, we got to the hilltop and saw some agriculture land. We laid low and sent two guys on a surveillance mission to find out where we were. They came back a short time later and said the area was safe. We were in the village of Hilaliyeh, a Druze village on our side. We walked more confidently uphill. Soon, we ran into a cucumber field. We were starved; we ate them like it would be the last time we were allowed to eat. We then sat on the rocky ground while the guy with the wireless communication contacted the leadership and informed them of our location. The leadership instructed us to stay put. They sent a bus to pick us up.

While waiting, one of the fighters had turned on his transistor radio to a Palestinian radio station broadcast. The announcer of the news proudly proclaimed, "Our fighters cleansed Monte Verde of the Kataeb-fleeing forces. Our forces are well on their way to Tal Zaatar. This is the Voice of Palestine."

We looked at each other in dismay. Our faces and our posture had that defeated look. This was a shameful thing to hear. A big part of the news broadcast on the Voice of Palestine was more propaganda than actual news.

A short time later, a bus arrived. Many of the other fighters and I got on it and went back to regional headquarters. From there, some of us headed back to Sabra. Raji took us in his car. He was a leader responsible for Tanzim security. Tanzim was the organized students, workers, and women volunteers which we were part of. Raji was also from Tal Zaatar. He was pushing hard for any kind of action which might help the camp under siege, even if it was not so well planned. The Monte Verde operation was another one of those poorly planned activities which cost lives and only resulted in disappointment and failure. It did not end at that. A couple of weeks later, Raji sent for me. I went to see him, and he asked that I join another group heading to Monte Verde again. I was shocked. I responded, "When we went the first time, Kataeb did not expect we would infiltrate that far. We still could not make it and retreated with casualties. A second time would only be suicidal. I'm sorry, I won't go there again." He did not pressure me to go, and I left.

A couple of weeks later, I knew there were other attempts to reach Tal Zaatar through Monte Verde, which failed as well. I also learned that Adnan, the dark quiet guy, was killed in one of those attempts. I'm not sure his body was ever recovered. Only a handful of fighters made it into the camp. They infiltrated on their own, one or two at a time through the mountains, and went undiscovered. One of them was Ibrahim, a friend who survived it all. Getting into the camp did not make much difference, however; it only helped the morale of people in the camp that perhaps there was a hope after all.

Attacks on the camp only became fiercer, until finally the camp fell. The few fighters who remained alive, got out of the camp, fighting their way through the mountains. From there, they headed to Beirut. On August 12, 1976, the camp was empty of Palestinian fighters. Kataeb and their allies, namely, the Guardians of the Cedars, Numur al-Ahrar (Tiger forces of the free), and others, went into the camp killing everyone they could at random. There were so many women, elderly, and children that they just fled en masse out of the camp. Some were killed, but many of them made their way through East Beirut toward West Beirut. The Beirut Museum was the last spot before they would walk into West Beirut.

Along with others, I heard the news that day. Someone had called me and suggested taking a truck and heading to the museum to meet the survivors. A friend and I went down on the street in Sabra, stopped an 18-wheeler open truck, and asked the driver if he was interested in helping. He agreed, and we got on the truck and headed to the cross point.

Shortly afterward, they arrived, a walking crowd— screaming, wailing, crying—they looked like they had been buried underground and somehow managed to get out. I was looking with shock and astonishment until they got near me. The truck was backed up and ready, and other trucks, as well. They looked at me with such scared eyes. They did not talk to me, did not talk to anyone. They looked like they had seen the devil in action.

I yelled, "I am a Palestinian! I came to help take you to a safe place." The adult women climbed onto the truck. I carried the children and elderly and put them on the truck. The truck filled up fast. I was amongst them. I told the driver to go. It felt like doomsday was upon us. Mothers and wives were calling out the names of their loved ones who were killed on the road to the museum. "They shot him in the head," "they dragged her away from me," "they just shot and killed on the street." I heard them cry and shout out, along with names, "My son . . ." It was a day I will never forget.

A caravan of trucks headed toward a teachers' college. It was on summer break. On the way, people of West Beirut lined the street sides. People on balconies and in cars . . . Everyone stopped and looked at the people in the trucks with shock and sympathy. It was like seeing what a true disaster looks like.

Many trucks arrived at Dar il Mualimeen, as the college was called. They all went into a large hall. Relatives who were in West Beirut came, hoping to meet surviving relatives from the fallen camp. I ran into my eighth-grade math teacher, Khair. He looked worried and scared. He told me he was looking for his brother and his brother's family. I did not say a word. There was no way he was going to find his brother. There were no adult men among the crowd. They were either killed in the camp or on the way to West Beirut.

In later years, I met a survivor, a brother of a friend. He told me he was one of the people who were on the trucks. He survived only because he was very short for his age. Otherwise, any boy of 14 or older was shot on the spot in front of his mother, sisters, and younger brothers. He told me there was a Christian Lebanese woman, whose son was a fighter and killed in the battle of Tal Zaatar. She carried a pistol, just selected Palestinians at random, and shot them dead. Some Kataeb and Christian right-wing fighters kidnapped Palestinian girls to rape them, and then kill them afterward. It was a mass killing hysteria. Between 3,000 to 4,000 Palestinians were massacred in Tal Zaatar.

The largest number of Tal Zaatar refugees were sent to resettle in none other than the evacuated town of Damour, that lasted until years later when the PLO was driven out of Lebanon, and the Christian right ruled. It was payback time again, so they were kicked out and were disbursed in many different areas of Lebanon and the world.

Syrian Army Ruling Beirut

Within a couple of months, the Syrian army was well spread out throughout Lebanon. In Beirut, Syrian forces circled many quarters. They set up bases in the heart of the city and in a great many of its districts, including the financial district and the hotels quarter. They set up checkpoints on the main roads and checked identities of passersby. They had lists of people wanted by them. A person with his name on such lists would be arrested and from there, most likely was transported to a jail in Syria. The Syrian regime was well-known for being ruthless with its prisoners. They might not ever be seen again by their relatives unless they were set free some years later. Syrian forces became the new rulers of Lebanon, while the Palestinian and Lebanese factions shrank to their closely held quarters and neighborhoods. That year, Lebanon was unofficially occupied by Syria with a full mandate from the Arab League of states, and indirectly or privately was accepted by Western countries, including the U.S. All these countries wanted to see an accountable party in charge in Lebanon which housed the PLO and Lebanese national factions. They did not want foreign leftist factions or opposition organizations that made Beirut their base as it would cause future threats and conflicts.

Kamal Jumblat Assassination

The dream of a progressive, democratic regime in Lebanon was also killed during that time. The symbolic and active leader of that dream, Kamal Jumblat, a most popular leader of the Lebanese National Movement and greatly beloved, was assassinated while in his car. An enormous amount of bullets were fired at his car which killed him and his bodyguards on the spot. The Syrian regime was blamed by all Jumblat supporters, including the PLO and all other Lebanese National Movement factions, however, none of them announced it publically for fear of a deadly retaliation by the Syrian regime. The assassins did not leave a trace. No serious investigation was ever conducted, so all accusations were based on assumed motives. The hit was a professional one, well planned, and no real evidence or proof was ever presented to support whether the Syrian regime perpetuated the killing of the Lebanese popular leader or whether it was some other party interested in feeding the fires of

Lebanon. However, hatred of Jumblat by the Syrians was quite apparent and well-known. I witnessed gunmen of the Saeqa Palestinian faction of the Syrian Baath party spray painting the outside walls of the Arab university of Beirut a block or two away from Arafat's headquarters office, with short statements calling Jumblat a "Zionist agent" for criticizing Hafez Assad's policies in Lebanon.

Battling the Syrian Army at the Doorsteps of the PLO

Syrian checkpoints created a restrictive obstacle and limited the flow of movement between PLO and Lebanese National Movement-controlled locations. Pressure continued to mount until a clash erupted. One afternoon, all PLO fighters were called to their bases. From there, a great many were stationed in fighting positions on the borders of Palestinian camps and supporting Lebanese neighborhoods which had no Syrian army presence. We were told the Syrian regime decided to totally contain and control the Palestinian revolution and the PLO. Familiar street panic scenes occurred: cars racing by, people at the grocery stores buying all they could afford to purchase, people rushing to their homes, and streets becoming vacant of civilians.

I drove my mother to a relative's home in a neighborhood which was unlikely to be a battleground. My younger sister was a nurse assistant volunteer at a shelter building of the Arab university of Beirut which turned into a Palestinian fighters' hospital, and I went back to our base. For the next few days, fierce fighting took place. It was the toughest I had lived through. We defended our positions, especially our base which was faced by Syrian Special Forces, well-known at the time for their skills and advanced fighting equipment. We faced heavy barrages of rockets, several falling and exploding in a small radius. Those rockets did not just make a hole in a building—they took down an entire level of a building, or sheared a two-story building in half. Syrian forces did not try to advance on us, they just gave us a good lesson of what it could be like if fighting continued.

We were nervous despite our strong fighting spirit. During that battle, Nidal rode with me in an open Jeep. We were heading to get ammunition from behind a building exposed to Syrian forces. I put it in manual gear and took off so fast, instead of making it faster in crossing the dangerous street, however, the Jeep was spinning in the middle of the street while Nidal was holding on to the top iron bar of the Jeep. I tried to control the car while Syrian bullets flew over us. I finally did and got the Jeep to the other side. I did not know how I did it, but I was glad those few seconds did not turn into a nightmare . . . or worse.

Once we made it, comrade fighters stationed across the street who witnessed me struggling with the Jeep clapped their hands and saluted me for keeping control and not just stop the Jeep and jump out of it. During those few days, Nidal fought so hard and so reckless, I thought to myself he was asking to be killed. I saw him in wide open streets totally exposed to the Syrian Special Forces fire a rocket, then pull his Kalashnikov and shoot like there was no one around; he was totally crazy, and I was very mad at him and told him how he was being stupid and tried to shake him, to no avail. A couple of days later, a truce agreement was reached. Our close group all survived that fight unharmed. A few of our comrades at the base got shot, but still survived. The cease-fire held except for minor skirmishes in different hot spots and streets of opposing communities. Beirut was a quiet place for a change; it looked sad, electricity was hardly provided, municipal services were minimal, but the airport opened more steadily as days went by.

Our mood was down as we felt defeat and Syrian pressure all around. We tried to make the best out of that time. Fakhri came back from Russia and rejoined us. We also met new friends. They were also Fatah activists. Nidal became their roommate. We got together more in the evenings for drinks, listened to music and poetry, and we had girlfriends who joined our gatherings. The girls were also revolutionaries. The country was trying to restore basic daily living requirements; however, anyone who was not politically committed wanted to leave and live abroad . . . make a life away from death and destruction which was all around us.

During a very short exchange of fire in Shayah, Barakat, a comrade and a friend of Nidal and his roommates was shot in his abdomen. He was laid up in one of Beirut's hospitals. Four of us took turns staying next to his bed and keeping him company and made sure he was getting the proper hospital care. He did not speak a word for many nights and was often in pain. We did not know if Barakat would make it. One night during my turn, and in the early-morning hours, to my shock, Arafat and Hasan Salameh, with no prior notice, walked into the room. Arafat came close to Barakat's hospital bed, greeted him, and said, "How are you, Hero?" He noticed Barakat's abdomen wounds and continued, "These are all medals, all of them medals."

Suddenly, Barakat was able to talk and smile. He said, "I am good, Brother Abu Ammar."

Arafat asked him if he needed anything. Barakat asked for water, which he was not allowed to have. Arafat looked around and said, "Water, water, get him water." The nurse interfered to say it was not good for him to drink water; after all, he was being nourished through his veins. Arafat told Barakat to be patient until he recovered enough to drink water. Arafat then greeted us and left with his companions. The next day I shared the story of Arafat's visit with Nidal and our friends, and more importantly, of how Arafat had the magic to bring back Barakat's ability to talk and smile. Barakat recovered in few weeks, and we kept on reminding him and teasing him about Arafat's hospital visit for months after.

Lebanon Civil War Destruction

Chapter 8

After the War, and PLO Plan Diversion

Beirut was trying to regain some of its lively spirit, however, war aftermath was everywhere. The downtown was totally destroyed, rubble lay on the streets, great historic architecture buildings became skeletons, garbage was strewn everywhere, feral dogs and cats prowled without fear, the streets were deserted and scary, street pavement everywhere was filled with large potholes, electricity was hardly available, and drinking water was scarce. However, we felt the truce was going to hold this time, mainly because there was a new sheriff in town and that was the Syrian army. Somehow, we all felt the civil war, and all its dead and wounded, and the communities which were cleansed and dislocated, and those who left the country—all that was for nothing. There was no change to the Lebanese religious sectarian regime. The Palestinian revolutionary forces had become contained and mostly surrounded by the Syrian forces on one side and had to deal with the Israeli army in the south of

190

Lebanon. Freedom of movement around Lebanon as well as in and out of Lebanon had become controlled by the Syrian intelligence. They even had full control of Beirut's international airport as well as all other border points of entry and exits out of the country.

We tried to ignore all that environment. We met more in evenings, we drank, we had more time to spend with our girlfriends, however, we all felt life became different. Reality hit hard for everyone. The war seemed over, and suddenly we had to figure out what to do with our lives. Nidal tried to lose himself in socializing during the day and getting drunk at night. Fakhri, recently back from Russia, joined us and told us his story of falling in love with Natasha, a beautiful girl in Moscow, a romance which seemed to have left him heartbroken. Eventually he adjusted back to reality that his trip to Russia was not supposed to last for life. A couple of months later, he managed to find a local girl and romance budded and he regained his original feelings of belonging with us.

Some of the guys got into the habit of smoking hash; others got more passionately involved in the internal debates and lectures. Many Fatah proclaimed thinkers and intellectual leaders were delivering lectures, evaluating the events which took place. They presented their ideas of where the Palestinian movement should be heading thereafter. Many ideas were being thrown around, from the extreme Marxist Leninist to the religious advocates . . . from those who called for strengthening the armed struggle, building up the Palestinian fighting capabilities, to those who called for minimizing that and just get engaged in a negotiated peace process.

Palestinian Compromises

A political plan which was adopted by the PLO in mid-1974 found new momentum when guns in Lebanon became relatively quiet. It was commonly known as the ten points program. It was the first documented change to the PLO covenant which called for the total liberation of historic Palestine. The ten point program proposed an interim solution, by which the Palestinians would agree to establish a state on any part of Palestine, whether liberated or obtained as a result of Israeli withdrawal. That was the punch line, enough to give the PLO leadership a launching pad to engage first indirectly through the Arab states, namely Saudi Arabia, a close friend of the U.S. and Egypt, which was on friendship terms with not only the U.S. but also European countries, the initiators and sponsors of the proposed peace plan to end the Palestinian and Arab conflict with Israel.

The then 2-year civil war gave the Palestinian leadership a dose of reality that Southern Lebanon was never going be their Vietnam-like forests, and Lebanon was not a comfortable supporter of the Palestinian military and political base. An interim solution became more appealing to the PLO leadership. Of course, the leadership would never present any change to young active followers like myself and my comrades or to the Palestinian people as a change due to weakness and lack of vision. They presented change as a new and innovative political maneuvering, while privately, they told us that liberating Palestine as a whole was the mission—that we will achieve the interim state and not recognize Israel or give away the right of return of all Palestinian refugees. It did not matter who the leader speaking to us in a political lecture was, whether from the right of Fatah known for their willingness to compromise on what is considered Palestinian inalienable rights, or from the left wing, which was more solid in adhering to the original covenants of Fatah and the PLO. Both spoke of the interim future state as some kind of prize the Palestinians will get based on their victories to that date. Each of them would present it in such a positive way and connect it to the future, which would be the ongoing struggle to liberate the rest of historical Palestine.

The reality was that my generation had no stomach to accept anything short of historic Palestine. However, my generation was too young at the time to understand the backdoor politics and negotiations which took place. "Maneuvering" was such a common term in Fatah that a great many of us accepted that Yasser Arafat was *maneuvering* politically. As long as he brought us more guns and allowed us to fight, his maneuvering was aimed at confusing the enemy and bringing us more support from those moderate states that wanted to hear the peace process was progressing forward and we, the Palestinians, were part of it. That was how the most senior leaders of Fatah and the PLO marketed their compromises, and most of us bought it, although some were very skeptical. I was one of those. However, most skeptics kept criticism constructive. We never imagined that from that point on, the course of Palestinian politics was changing.

As part of the public debate, many speeches were being delivered in person by the top leaders of the largest factions. In a speech by Dr. George Habash, the well respected leader of the Popular Front for the Liberation of Palestine, I was sitting up so close to the stage and remember he was mad and angry and could not keep his cool while he explained that a state in the West Bank and Gaza was a crazy idea. "What state are they talking about? Such a small area of Palestine has no potential to become a state. Why should we accept a little part of our country?"

However, most Fatah leaders spoke differently. They justified it as a means to be able to engage with and build stronger relations with most of the influential states in the world, including, at the time, the Soviet Union, who wanted to see a two-state solution. In our Fatah cadre meetings, a leader from the first circle of leadership was usually invited to speak to us. He would argue that without a flexible strategy, the PLO, and therefore the Palestinian cause, would become an outcast to most of the world.

Factions who rejected such a plan formed a coalition and called it the "Rejection Front," and that plan divided the Palestinians. Many small battles erupted between Fatah and its follower factions on one side, and the Rejection Front on the other. The Palestinian street became tense; people argued everywhere. Somehow, Arafat's leadership was very confident of achieving the two-state solution as an interim solution. However, things did not work out that way.

Back to School

Months passed by. Schools reopened. I went to register for my Lebanese high school, but I had a psychological problem. After 2 years of chaos, I felt I grew up too fast. I had too much power during the war. I had experienced authority. How would I obey a teacher in a classroom, or a school vice principal who would control my behavior? It was very hard. I had the choice of ending my education right there and then and continue as a full-time activist, fighter, and pursue higher positions within Fatah, or humble myself and conform to school rules. I pushed myself to adopt the latter choice.

It was a short and compacted education year. At the end of the school year, we were assigned the date of the official state exam. Students of that grade took the exam the same day. The Ministry of Education, which was responsible for setting up the exam date and the exam material, also assigned a different school where the exams were taken, which was not the same school the student attended during the school year. The problem was that those assigned school locations were across the warring sections of the Lebanese cities and towns. I did not know what to think of that, or why they made such decisions, but the students had no choice. No show meant failing the grade.

My assignment for the exam, along with my classmates, was in Furn el Chebbak. When I heard that I was shocked. That is a major neighborhood in East Beirut, and it was a huge Kataeb area. I thought to myself, a Lebanese from West Beirut, going to East Beirut during a truce, may be tolerated by the Kataeb and their allies; however, for a Palestinian, it was a different story. If discovered, his life might become history.

The day of the exam came, and I was very nervous. Nidal and two of our comrades decided to accompany me in a car and gave me a ride to the Furn el Chebbak High School, where I was assigned to take my exam. Crazy as we were, we loaded the car with Kalashnikovs and hand grenades, and off we drove . . . right into East

Beirut. There were no checkpoints for the Lebanese army or any other force. I guess they wanted to make that day look and feel peaceful.

We arrived with no problems. I got off at the school gate, and they went back. That first day went well. Nidal and my friends came back at the end of the day and picked me up, and we went back to Sabra. The next day was a break, to be followed by the second day of the official state exam. That break day was not a break for me, however. Nidal, my buddy, was so much in love with a girl, he had met her parents to get engaged. Her name was Faten. They refused. Nidal and his girlfriend decided to get married despite her family's objection, and they decided to do it wherever the girl would run away with him. Getting married that way in Lebanon has a strange term: "*khateefeh.*" The exact translation is "kidnapping"; however, it is not really kidnapping, it is eloping, since both the potential groom and bride plan and conduct it together. Well, Nidal's parents' home was in Damascus, Syria. He wanted to send his girlfriend there. He himself couldn't go because his identification papers were messed up and needed time to get fixed. Somehow, he did not believe he had time. He thought his girlfriend might be under too much pressure to accept an engagement to another guy who was more suitable, at least by her parents' standards. Nidal insisted on me accompanying his girl to Damascus on the break day between my two-day exams. Had I not accepted, I would have had to live with the guilt of causing him the loss of another love of his life. Not too thrilled, I accepted the task.

I met the girl for the first time along with Nidal, who introduced us. We took a taxi and started the few hours' trip out of the country into Syria. At the border crossing, the Lebanese officer called both me and the girl into his office. He questioned us, why we were together and why we were leaving the country. I told him that despite our different last names, our mothers, who hold different last names, were related, and my companion was going to visit relatives in Damascus. I was merely accompanying her for safety. Whether he bought the story or not, I did not know, but he let us continue on our way.

An hour and a half later, we were in Damascus. We arrived at Nidal's parents' home. Nidal's parents were very happy to see us upon our arrival. I knew that Nidal had called several times to find out if we had arrived. Coffee was served to us, and I took a sip or two. When Nidal called again, he asked for me and said, "I'm here with Abu Ilmakarim, the base commander." He then passed the phone receiver to him.

"We solved the issue with the Faten's family. Please come back and bring her with you," Abu Ilmakarim said. I assured him we would be on our way back.

I was so pissed, however. I whispered to Nidal, "You bastard, what is this all about? You got me crossing countries and you don't want to go through with it? What will happen to the girl? Her family might hurt her for doing this." Normally, if a girl eloped with the man she loved and got married, the marriage became a fact of life, and life went on. However, if the girl went back home right away, only God knows what might happen next. Abu Ilmakarim got on the phone again and told me that Faten's family gave him assurance the girl was safe with them if she went back. Given his status and position, that was a good assurance. Faten and I headed back to Beirut before dark. We parted ways shortly after we stepped out of the taxi. She went to her home, and I went back to get ready for the second part of my exam.

The next day I got my ride back to the same high school in East Beirut, went through many hours of exams, and just a few minutes before the last exam period ended, I heard gunfire from a distance. It started slow, then intensified and became louder. I finished my exam, turned in my papers, and left the school, heading to the main Furn el Chebbak Boulevard. I was very nervous. People on the street were in a hurry going places as the gunfire resumed. I was walking fast, and suddenly, a few feet ahead of me, a Kataeb fighter was standing right on the curb with his uniform missing a green shirt. He wore a white T-shirt and his beret with the Kataeb logo. The Kataeb office was right across the street. Thoughts rushed through my head. I felt almost defenseless and helpless about what could happen next. Given my long hair look of the times, my beard and jeans, I thought to myself, *Surely I'm a dead man.* It's amazing how thoughts race in seconds while a person is in danger. I thought if I turn and went back the opposite way, I was going to raise more suspicion, so I kept just walking.

A person passed by me and asked me what time it was. With a fake Lebanese accent I told him I didn't know and kept on walking. I almost brushed my right shoulder with the Kataeb fighter's big belly, the guy was so big. I walked past him while still thinking that he might call me to question me at any moment, but he did not. I walked faster, turned left on a crossroad leading to the west, walked faster yet, but without looking scared. I tried to look like I was from the neighborhood. I knew that snipers were on their way to their positions, about half a kilometer short of a road separating the fighting parties of the east and the west. Now I started running. I ran as fast as I could, and I tried not to be exposed to snipers, but, of course, there was no way I could do that, so I just ran in a zigzag fashion and ducked below the side walls and continued while I felt like a bird in the open and expected to be hit at any moment by a sniper watching a guy running alone in the empty street to West Beirut. Just when the exchange of fire started, I had made it into a heavy tree area and felt secure enough to walk the rest of the way to my neighborhood.

Weeks passed, and finally, the results of the national exams were announced. I passed. At least all that stress paid off.

The next academic school year was totally messed up. Much time was lost due to the war. The Ministry of Education made up for some of the lost time by compressing the second and final baccalaureate, precollege year. This is an extra year high school students have in Lebanon to aid them in determining whether they would choose to be in literature, art, or have a scientific and mathematic emphasis. I chose science.

The academic year was completed in less than half the usual time, and official tests were to be conducted in the local community high schools, unlike the first time, where the students tested in the schools located outside their community neighborhoods. They did not need to go to the other side of town now. The tests were unusually easy, unlike previous years, and only a small percentage of students failed. I was very happy that I passed and was ready to apply and join a university.

I applied to the American University of Beirut, however, my family did not want me to stay in Beirut, especially after many episodes of renewed fighting, whether with the Lebanese Christian right, or in the south of Lebanon, where Israeli incursions took a different turn by creating their own force with Lebanese members led by a Lebanese army officer called Saad Haddad, who split from the Lebanese army and declared the establishment of South Lebanon Army (SLA), which later was renamed to Free Lebanon Army. It was very obvious that it relied on Israel for its support, both militarily and financially. It was stationed in certain towns until it became clear what role Israel had in store for it. It was to create a geographic zone along the borders, totally controlled by Haddad's army, to prevent Palestinian fighters from infiltrating across the border. More important, it was to neutralize the growing Palestinian rocket arsenal by pushing it away, as far as possible, from the border's range. Haddad's army's doctrine was to free Lebanon from the Palestinians, killing any Palestinian, civilian, young, or old. This happened frequently. Battles with Free Lebanon Army became more frequent, and fighters from our group were sent to the south to engage in such fights.

In Beirut, street quarrels between frustrated fighters for personal reasons increased. Fights like that usually included pistols pulled out to threaten the adversary, even shooting in the air, and if things escalated, people were shot. I myself was involved in at least two of those fights. Tension was in the air, anything triggered a quarrel. The right of way for drivers, a simple car accident, even rubbing shoulders the wrong way or a focused look at someone's girlfriend, or, like in my case, someone obnoxiously tried to flirt with my younger sister Salma right after I dropped her off at a Red Crescent center where she volunteered as a nurse . . . well, I came out of the car. He was a fighter with another Palestinian faction. I showed him my dismay and told him that he needed to have some manners. Instead of apologizing, he came at me arrogantly and tried to push me when I grabbed his arm. I pulled him to my side while I blocked his foot. He fell facedown. Knowing he had a pistol by his side, and I did, it was only a matter of time before he would pull it, so I beat him to it. I pulled my Tokarev Russian-made pistol and fired a shot at the floor near him. A friend of his was with him and tried to calm me down. I did not trust him and pushed him away. Before I knew it, I was surrounded by at least 10 people who tried to calm me into putting my gun away; a few were around him too. As soon as I did and my adversary saw that, he pulled his gun and put it to my head. The others then began to calm him down. Then he put his gun back on his side, and we both were pulled apart. That happened in the heart of Fakahani. Around us were multistory apartment buildings, which housed many Fatah offices. Toward the end of the fight I remember glancing at a balcony right above where the fight was taking place, and I saw Abu Saleh, a Fatah founder and military leader. He was talking to his assistants and looking at me and my adversary. I got to know Abu Saleh years later, but never brought up the incident.

Chapter 9

Life-Changing Trip, Leaving for America

Muhannad, while in Texas, obtained a university admission approval for me. I received it in Beirut in the summer of 1977. Once my family knew of it, they encouraged me to follow up on it by trying to get a student visa from the U.S. Embassy and travel there. To them, it was the best thing I could do, since they rightfully believed my life was in constant danger. I was feeling the frustration of where our lives, along with our cause, were heading. I saw nothing but decline, and I felt we were as far from Palestine and its true cause as was America. Anyway, I felt our homeland, our history, everything I believed in was being sold out due to failures and defeats of the Palestinian revolution. I lost faith in the Palestinian leadership represented by Arafat. I did not foresee better achievements ahead. Instead, I just saw a lot of sugarcoating of bitter pills. To me, accepting less than a democratic, historical Palestine was a sellout. Now, I thought leaving was not such a bad idea. Perhaps Fatah would straighten out its leadership and get back on track. After all, there were many leaders as well as many cadres who did not agree with Arafat's line of thinking and strategy for peaceful settlement with Israel based on two states.

I came home one afternoon, rushed to remove my shoes by pushing one shoe off using my other foot, and then using my bare foot to push the other shoe off. My old aunt was watching my shoes land one on top of the other. She smiled and looked at me and said, "You will be traveling." It was some kind of superstition, one of many in our culture for predicting good, bad, or major events in life, similar to reading one's fortune from images and symbols from leftover coffee grains in a Turkish coffee cup after it had been tipped upside down. It's amazing how we were tempted to believe what a coffee cup fortune-teller says. The fortune-teller was usually a woman, a relative or some neighbor. Of course, they had some vague record behind them of predictions which came true. Often, people paid money to proclaimed fortune-tellers with famous reputations in Beirut or elsewhere in Lebanon, not just to predict, but also to help them solve a problem or improve their life situations in a mystical way. These particular fortune-tellers claimed to have a relationship with genies which could make things happen.

A few days later, I prepared my paperwork, including my travel documents in lieu of a normal passport. Just like all Palestinian refugees in Lebanon, that document was the closest one I could get to a passport. I went to the American Embassy in Beirut, applied for a visa, even though I did not have high hopes. I thought my beard, long hair, jeans, and serious look, on top of living in Sabra, would give me away as a typical young political activist. It was a common look and well associated with Palestinian and Lebanese young active cadres. To my surprise, it did not matter to the American consul. He asked me a couple of questions about my study plans in the U.S., and asked me to leave my travel documents and come back in few hours. I did, and when I returned, I got my passport and saw a granted visa stamped in it. I was thrilled and stunned at the same time. Right there and then was a life-changing event. I was more prepared to be turned down than to be approved. After all, we had a love-hate relationship with America.

I did not know what to think. The idea of traveling so far, staying away for years was a sobering thought. But it was really happening. I felt somber.

Thoughts of physically separating from Beirut and all my loved ones, family, friends, the Palestinian people, and the genuine feeling of being part of the struggle for Palestine made me sad. I had to adjust to that new dimension of my life. However, my mind was not totally made up. I was not sure I wanted to do it. Many people in Beirut at that time thought I was crazy to even hesitate. They just did not see staying as a comparable alternative. It would not even come close to providing an opportunity to improve my life like in such a great place like the U.S., which had so much to offer a young man. My older sister Suhair encouraged me to go. She always had a calming effect on me, and I trusted her opinion; she convinced me that it was a great thing for me to leave and see the world out there, as opposed to staying in a limited place caught in wars and chaos like Beirut.

I spent the next few weeks with my family, especially my brother Walid and my sisters, who were in Beirut for a summer vacation. They wanted to be with me before my planned travel. Walid was not only encouraging, he took on the financial responsibility of my university tuition and my living expenses in the U.S., something I lived to deeply appreciate. I was so grateful for his help and support. He gave me a chance he himself did not get. I wrapped up my few affairs in Beirut within a few days, bought an airline ticket, said good-bye to everyone I cared about, and prepared for my departure.

The day of my flight was so emotional. My grandmother had more than tears of separation in her eyes. I saw great sadness. She hugged me as hard as she could for an old woman. She was saying good-bye for the last time. Somehow, I felt strongly I would not see her again.

I left for the airport and got on a plane for the first time in my life. I looked out the little window while the plane took off. I could not get enough of looking at Beirut from the air and bid it farewell. I departed with nostalgic feelings regarding my life—my childhood, my teenage years, my struggles, my attachment to a very special city where I felt intense happiness and sadness. I recalled the many parties, weddings, and too many funerals I had attended. I had walked most of its streets in the summer and under rain. Revolutionary Beirut was a utopia. I loved it. My friends and I fought so hard to defend it, and some of them paid with their lives or a dear price to keep it the way it evolved because of our sacrifices. To me and to many Palestinian and Lebanese young revolutionaries, it was a place where revolution, freedom, idealism, love, poetry, music, and the beauty of simplicity came together.

My thought was never to immigrate to create a new life. All I wanted was to get my education, get some experience from a culture and a society far advanced in many aspects. I wanted to become an engineer, go back to Beirut, contribute on a different level, maybe build shelters to protect innocent people of the refugee camps from air bombardments and constant shelling from East Beirut during intense fighting. Perhaps build hospitals or schools. I was not one of those who thought of getting a job and accumulating money. Palestine was in my blood and felt more like an addiction; my life revolved around it, and I could not imagine being away from the struggle for it. I wanted to be more active and make a difference.

My first stop from Beirut was Prague, the capital of Czechoslovakia. I had to transit to a Czechoslovakian airline from there to New York. Even in the transit, I had to pass through a checkpoint of airport security. It was my first introduction to seeing how a Palestinian was treated in international airports. Once the security officer saw my travel documents, he asked me to step aside and pointed to the spot where he instructed me to go. There, I was fully searched while all other passengers passed by, then I was questioned as to the motives of my travel. When I showed my U.S. student visa, my story was verified and I was allowed to pass through.

Walking in the airport of a different country was strange to me. People did not speak Arabic or English. My English was not so bad, except for the heavy English accent we learned in schools. Somehow, however, I made it to the gate for the plane, where I waited, and then followed the crowd into it. It was not as big a plane as I imagined it would be; only three seats on each side. The passengers were seated. There was only one flight attendant who was really a little freaky and nervous all the time, which made me feel I had embarked on a risky trip. She would say to the passengers, "You need to be seated." "Don't move." "We are going to cross the ocean," etc., and the way she behaved, I felt there was a good chance we were going to end up in the ocean, rather than cross it.

A few hours into the flight, we went through some rough air turbulence, something I had never experienced before, and no one ever told me about it or bumpy flights. I thought to myself for sure something was wrong with the plane. That attendant did not help. Her face and demeanor continued to show her nervousness. It was a long and tiring flight. People were allowed to smoke on planes then, so everyone other than the smokers was forced breathe secondhand smoke. A man who was seated in the row in front of me pulled out and lit a cigar, which made the freaky attendant even freakier. She came shouting, "You can't do that. You're not allowed to smoke cigars on the plane, only cigarettes." She took the cigar from him and went to put it out somewhere. Despite my many later flights, I still remember that flight as the longest and most agonizing I ever experienced.

We arrived in New York at the airport. I was stunned with how gigantic the place was. Then I was thinking of how violent that city was, and that one could be robbed or shot anywhere. All these American movies I watched and news about New York caused me to be extremely cautious at the airport. I was carefully watching people walking by me. It was past midnight. Panic was added to my disorientation. While sitting in front of the boarding gate, I realized I did not have my small leather handbag with me. In it I had a cashier's check for a few thousand dollars, given to me be my brother Walid to start my student life in America, along with my travel documents. For a horrible moment, I thought disaster struck upon my arrival. I went running to the ticket counter, where I realized I left it, but by then, no one was at the counter. The employees were all gone for the night. However, my small tan leather handbag was laying right there on the counter. I grabbed it and felt a huge wave of relief wash over me. Many thoughts came to mind during those couple of terrifying minutes, like what will happen to me with no money and no travel document, which was the only personal identification I had. How vulnerable one's life can be due to the simple act of leaving a small bag behind!

 I checked into my flight heading to Dallas. I knew the United States was a big country, but one can especially see how big it is compared to Lebanon (a little over 10,000 square kilometers) when flying over it. I looked out my window at dawn, and all I could see was a huge expanse of land, mostly uninhabited. I thought to myself, how ironic . . . all that empty land and no one was fighting over it, while Palestine, that tiny place in comparison, had endless wars being fought over it.

I arrived in Dallas, Texas, and took a taxi to the University of Dallas. Along the way, I noticed vast distances between buildings, something I never saw coming from a place like Beirut, where buildings were packed closely together. I was especially surprised with the university size and its great many large buildings.

I headed to the international student center, where they sent me to the dormitory building. There I met Ali, an old friend from Beirut, who came there a few months before. I was totally jet-lagged and just needed to sleep, which I did. I woke up a few hours later and together with Ali, went to the cafeteria. Everything was strange to me; even the salad dressing was strange. I had no clue what "thousand islands" was or how it tasted, like when they asked me if that was what I wanted on my salad. I looked at Ali who nodded for me to say yes, so I did. Shortly after, I learned that Muhannad had moved to California. That was a blow to me for I was counting on him to guide me and help put me on the right track as I had no idea where to start in the American system. I was overwhelmed and lost. Ali helped explain to me how I needed to start, and that the university admission I had in my hands was conditional to joining the university language center where my English language level would be assessed, and I would be informed of the program I needed to complete, which meant I could easily spend a year studying the language through the various levels required by the university. I did not like that since I had passed an American language test with an acceptable score to allow me into a university. From the start, I had to correct my visa status and get accepted by a university.

It was now October, and almost halfway through the semester. One evening, two guys I knew from Beirut, Ghassan and Mutasim, came by. It was a nice surprise to see them, especially Mutasim who was a distant friend. They told me they were in Dallas for the weekend. We went out to a nightclub, where I felt strange and out of place. My newly met friends were already familiar with Texan Americans. They even spoke English with a Southern accent. I did not know how to have any conversation with the all-American girls, many, of whom, wore cowgirl hats, jeans, and boots, the same thing as the guys, who my friends knew and invited to our table. I also felt my overly serious look on my face might not be very friendly to them either. However, my new friends were very nice. They welcomed me into their group and quickly made me feel more at ease with the place. We started sharing some laughter along with some drinks. That same weekend, they suggested I go with them to Oklahoma City, where they went to a college, so I joined them, along with Ali. We became four roommates for three months, after which Ali, who had some friends in the University of Mississippi, suggested we both go there since that university accepted the Lebanese baccalaureate which meant I would save a semester or two. I was eager to start and complete my undergraduate engineering studies, but I was in too much of a rush for my own good, especially for someone who was not fully aware of the American education system. Ali's friends helped us both get accepted at "Ole Miss," the nickname of the University of Mississippi, located near a town called Oxford.

In the first week of January, Dallas was covered in snow. By then I had bought a car, a Ford Mustang, and was getting ready to drive to Mississippi. Suddenly, Ali changed his mind and wanted to stay. I was going alone. Against everyone's advice that the road was too dangerous to drive across in the state, I was intent on going, being too stubborn and determined to leave. I just did not want to miss the registration deadline and miss a whole semester. I was loading my car when Ali waved at me through the apartment window and asked me to wait for him. He changed his mind again and wanted to join me. He threw his luggage in the trunk and got in the car with me, and I was glad he did. The weather conditions were extremely harsh. For the next 14 agonizing hours, I drove on icy, snowy highways. There were almost no other cars on the road. The highways were mostly deserted, with only a few trucks there, some, of which, had flipped over on their sides because of the ice. But I was still determined to go, even when my car occasionally slid from one side of the road to the other. It did not matter to me. I thought all that was easily manageable for someone who had come out of street warfare of Beirut. It was no big deal. That was the price to pay for waiting too long to decide to leave Dallas. We finally got there. It was late at night, but the dormitory manager accommodated us. The next morning we made it just in time and registered for the semester.

Walking around Ole Miss was enough to make me feel the tension of the place. People of different races and colors did not feel comfortable around each other. My first shock came in early morning when it was time to go to class. Coming out of my room on the eighth floor of the dormitory building, I got in the elevator with a few Caucasian students. The next stop a black student got in. I noticed the white students moved back in an obvious motion to distance themselves from the black student, thus avoiding any contact. I saw that behavior every morning for the rest of the semester. Some of the white students who found foreign students like myself interesting to talk to told me they thought blacks were biologically inferior to whites.

A couple of times, white girls would flirt with me. One girl passed her phone number to me written on a little piece of paper. When I called her, she wanted to talk and get to know me. However, when I asked to meet her, she told me she couldn't. When I asked why, she said if she was seen with a foreigner she would become an outcast by her white friends. It was considered a disgrace to go out with a foreigner. It was not as bad as being seen with a black man, but it came in second place. I was totally shocked. For the first time in my life, I felt I was in a place where I was considered inferior because of my race and ethnicity. Many incidents occurred while I walked to and from class. I would hear guys shouting from a window, "Go to the Middle East, camel jockey," or "Hey, sand nigger," or similar insults.

Once I met a girl at the student lounge. She was friendly and wanted to make conversation, which was unusual for local girls. But Susan wasn't local; she was from New York. We met over coffee and chatted.

One evening, two guys suggested we go out to the only nightclub in the small town, so we all dressed up and headed to the club. I drove my Mustang. The club had a dirt driveway and an unpaved parking lot which was filled with pickup trucks, the common ride for the people of the town. We walked inside. To my surprise, most of the people in it were American country people dressed in cowboy outfits, with skinny jeans, cowboy boots, beaded shirts, and big hats. Some hats even had feathers. I felt intimidated and little insecure. I was hoping it was a place where mostly students frequented, but that was not the case, which was disappointing. However, I did my best to get in the mood of the music and dancing while having a beer.

Ten minutes later, Susan happened to be in club. She came up to me to say hello and asked me to dance with her. I was happy to see a familiar face. I walked to the dance floor with her, danced a couple of songs, then a slow dance. By then, I noticed angry looks from a few of the cowboys around the dance floor, which I ignored. The song was over, I kissed her on the cheek and said good night. Shortly afterward, my friends and I left and walked toward my car. We got in the car, but as soon as I moved forward, three cowboys blocked my car by standing in front of it. One came to my side, another the passenger's side, and the third climbed on top of the car roof. The doors were locked, so they couldn't get in.

I rolled the window down just enough to talk to the drunk cowboy. I could tell he was blasted with alcohol. He said, "Look, we have some sand niggers here. Come on, let's have a fight."

I said, "Why fight? We are all having fun here."

He disregarded what I said and continued to pull hard on the door. While looking at him, I put the gear in first gear, and we just took off. All three of them jumped away from the car. I drove quickly toward the dormitory and was very angry. That incident was the breaking point for me. I decided to leave Mississippi which I considered a nightmare place for me. I thought to myself, who cares if it takes me more time to graduate. That's better than having to put up with a place where I feel hatred, around a lot of people who do not know much about the rest of the world. To them, foreigners were not welcome, and blacks were openly discriminated against.

One time, a KKK member asked to meet with me when he knew I was Palestinian. He said to me,

"We should work together; we have a lot in common. We hate the Jews, you hate the Jews." I explained to him that we don't hate the Jews. We have a serious problem with Zionism and their political aims in Palestine, which is very different from hating Jews. The KKK member did not like that, and we never met again.

Once I had a discussion with the dean of the School of Engineering. We had a good relationship, but that was due to a lot of effort on my side. Then the dean asked me about my national background. When I informed him that I was Palestinian, he immediately went on the attack. He said, "Why do your people kill civilians? Why do they hijack planes? Why did they kill athletes in Munich?"

I was totally caught off guard. I had never experienced such attacks on the Palestinians since I only lived in my own environment. I heard of the European and Western resentment toward Palestinian acts, but never encountered it face-to-face. I thought our plight to get our rights as Palestinians was unquestionable. I did not hear any sympathy from the dean, only attacks from someone who held a high status in his society. I explained to the dean the whole Palestinian story, and what drove some Palestinians to take that track.

Finally, he showed some understanding and support of the Palestinian cause.

Chapter 10

Activist in a tolerant but Not so Friendly America

Connecting with Fatah Supporters in the U.S.

I was in contact with Muhannad and informed him how unhappy I was and that I thought of moving to California right after the end of the semester. He was encouraging. Meanwhile, Muhannad was apparently connected to Fatah supporters in the U.S. A couple of weeks later, a Palestinian student told me there was a guest in town who was asking to see me. He did not know much about him. I went with him and met the guest whose name was Naeem, a Lebanese Ph.D. student at the time, who was one of the major Fatah supporters in the U.S. He told me he heard a lot of good things about me and wanted to meet me and explore how to get me involved in supporting the Palestinian cause in the U.S. I was hesitant, given my resentment toward Fatah's leadership in Beirut and all that I had been through. I only wanted to cooperate with Fatah supporters who shared my thoughts. I believed that we needed to overhaul that leadership, and a more solid, more effective leadership was needed. Naeem and I agreed to remain in contact, and I suggested that we meet again in California.

Welcome to Hotel California

Toward the end of the semester, I received a "B" grade from my professor of computer science. My grade was 99.8 out of a hundred. I met the professor and asked him if he would reconsider and make my grade an "A," instead given the score I earned. I told him it would help me since I was transferring to another state.

He said, "No, it's a 'B,' and I'm glad you're transferring. We don't like you foreigners here, and when you transfer, don't make your major engineering. You foreigners don't have what it takes to be engineers." I looked at him with great dismay. I didn't know what to say to someone who thought that way. I left his office and was reassured that I made the right decision to leave.

I loaded my Mustang with my personal belongings. That time I had another companion who wanted to move to California as well. It was Wael. We knew each other from Beirut. We went to the same high school, and we got along with each other well. Ali decided to go back to Texas, and he did. I drove heading to San Diego, California. For the next 3 days, we were on the highway, only stopping for gas and food and a little rest, then back on the road. We were eager to get to California, to open a new page in our life.

We crossed through Arizona at night. Right when we saw the sign saying that we were entering California, we played the Eagle's song, "Hotel California" very loud and sang along with it. Shortly after we crossed, there was a mountainous road which needed extra attention while driving. It was wide and straight and dark. I fell asleep while driving. Suddenly I woke up. My Mustang was turning in 360 degrees. I found myself in the dirt ditch between the opposite lanes of the highway, dusty and full of fear. I was totally shaken. I had fallen asleep at the steering wheel!

Wael apparently was already asleep. I had asked him an hour or so before to watch me so I didn't doze off. I did not think he would fall asleep first. An 18-wheeler truck was parked on the emergency lane. The driver came toward us and asked me if we were OK. I replied we were, and he proceeded to tell me that he was driving behind me and for the last 10 minutes before I drove into the ditch, my car was wavering from lane to lane. He had his lights blinking to warn any cars behind him on the highway, and luckily, there were no cars. At that time, traffic was extremely light.

I asked why he didn't blow his horn to catch my attention. He said even though he assumed I was asleep, he did not want to startle me, which might have caused me to crash or cause the car to turn over and flip. I thought the man just was not sure what to do since there was no easy answer to get me to wake up gently. I thanked him for doing his best.

Luckily, Wael and I were unhurt. My car did not have any damage, so I drove it out of the ditch and back on the highway. I drove slowly in the right lane. It was not too long before the lights from a highway patrol vehicle blasted behind me. I pulled the car over and parked in the emergency lane. The officer came toward me, checked my papers, and asked me if I had had any alcohol or drugs. I answered no and informed him that I had been driving for 2 days without getting any sleep. He told me that was a crazy thing to do, and then ordered me to pull over at the next exit and just sleep in the car till sunrise, and if he caught me on the highway before that, he would take me to jail. I complied. We slept for 2 or 3 hours, woke up, went to a restaurant for breakfast, and resumed our trip to San Diego, which was only an hour and half away.

I drove into San Diego from the east. I was so happy to be there. The gentle hills and moderate weather were very familiar to me. I was so happy that despite feeling exhausted and lacking sleep, all I wanted to do was to drive around the streets, which I did for a few hours. Muhannad was attending classes. By noon we connected and talked for some time, catching up on what had been happening since he left Beirut. People of San Diego were by far nicer and friendlier than others we had met so far, and it was comforting to see people with different ethnic backgrounds . . Caucasian, Mexican, African Americans, and Asian, amongst others.

It was not too hard to take a summer course, then enroll in a university. I spent the rest of the summer getting to know the city, enjoying its beautiful atmosphere, and most of all, its beaches. It was as close as I could have been to my Mediterranean environment, with friendly people and smiling faces everywhere.

Meanwhile, nothing much changed for my friends back in Beirut. Problems between the east and west sides of Beirut were calm, thanks to the Syrian army. However, south Lebanon's tensions were more and more on the rise. Problems with the Christian right South Lebanon Army (SLA) and their Israeli ally became almost a daily event. My friends were engaged on and off in battles with the SLA, which became the IDF's proxy army. Logistics, money, and planning were secured by the IDF. The fighting part was done by the SLA.

In 1978, the IDF carried out an invasion of the south and fought hard battles with Fatah and PLO forces. When a cease-fire was agreed between the fighting parties, the IDF stood at a line well into Lebanese territory. The Israeli government achieved its declared goal of controlling a territory separating Israel and the PLO fighters and called it a security zone. It included numerous towns and villages, mostly Shiite Lebanese and a few Christian Lebanese which was turned over to the SLA, which ruthlessly ruled the land and the people. My contact with Nidal and Fakhri in Beirut was through letters sent by regular postal service from the U.S. Beirut postal service was not so reliable. Many of my letters to them and vice versa were never received while life was going forward and changing for all of us.

A part of me wanted to live my age as a student—study, socialize, and party—and a bigger part of me was still attached to Beirut and the whole Palestinian struggling life package. I followed the news daily. I was torn between trying to adjust to my new life while mentally I was still living there. I felt I was a passing guest. Time would pass and before long, I would find myself ready to go back. That feeling was getting stronger, yet I interacted more with American students or the Americans in daily public life, and I continued to be amazed at how little Americans knew about Palestine or the Palestinians. I had to explain the story of Palestine almost every time I met a friendly person who made conversation with me and asked me which country I was from. As soon as I would said Palestine, the person would respond by asking, "Where is that country?" and I would start telling the story from before 1948. That person generally became sympathetic but was still confused.

Most Americans I met in California were nice, simple, friendly, and welcoming. I felt they mostly dealt with life easily, unlike people from my part of the world. I did not notice the heavy burden of life on their shoulders. I thought Californians were making the best out of their lives to be happy. I noticed they did not complain much. I grew up where most people complained about the difficulties of life. It was surprising to me and astonishing to me how these people seemed so happy. They did not take life seriously; they seemed optimistic about their future. They also had no clue of how third world people viewed American foreign policy at the time. Some were dumbfounded when they heard views they had never been exposed to before. They could not understand why Palestinians resent American foreign policy. It was big news when I told them America was providing Israel with planes and bombs that were killing many civilians in Lebanon and elsewhere. Most were only convinced that Israel was fighting to survive in the middle of all those Arab countries. One American sympathizer to Palestine told me "supporting Israel, to me, was like supporting David against Goliath . . . until I found out that David actually had a nuclear bomb."

It was very hard to present the Palestinian cause without confronting that preconceived idea most Americans held. Americans who understood and supported Palestinians' national rights were easily confused and quick to reverse when they read or heard news coverage about Palestinian fighters infiltrating borders and killing Israelis. The American media generally had very negative coverage of Palestinians. The Palestinian plight for their homeland had no chance of support by Americans, and it was almost never presented based on our history, only Jewish and Israeli history. This was the first time in my life I felt I was in a place where people did not know or understand the Palestinian story. At the same time, it seemed ironic because the U.S. was, by far, the biggest supporter of Israel of all the Western countries involved in the Middle East affairs.

It took only a few months for me to be connected with Fatah supporters in the U.S. Muhannad arranged a meeting in Sacramento for both of us with Amjad, the chairman, elected by supporters. Fatah was not accepted in the U.S., and neither was the PLO. They were classified as terrorist organizations. However, the U.S. government seemed to have accepted an indirect presence of both, and other Palestinian factions, while officially never recognizing any of them. In order not to have much trouble, Fatah made its presence unofficial. The key was in the word "supporters"; somehow, Fatah activists believed if they were only supporters, rather than full members, it would save them unpleasant clashes with the U.S. government bodies. Fatah and the PLO supporters in the U.S. believed their role was to play a public relations role, to help prepare for a U.S. recognition of the PLO and Fatah as well.

Muhannad and I drove to Sacramento. First, we met with Saber, who was the chief coordinator of the Fatah supporters of the western U.S. region. That evening, all three of us went to Amjad's home. I was told he had just recently moved to Sacramento. At that time, I was not convinced, yet, I wanted to join Fatah supporters in the U.S., mainly because I did not know what their position was toward the political settlement Arafat's leadership was trying to achieve with Israel. Fatah included many schools of thought. They acted like organizations within an organization. They were groups of Fatah individuals who found each other to be leaning toward a certain ideology. They had their own views. Some were considered leftists, and the others were rightists. None were unified. The leftists were a few clusters, and the rightists were also a few clusters. They all had differences, political and ideological. Leftists mostly believed in Russian and Chinese communists as their models; rightists were considered capitalists or allies of what leftists considered as reactionary Arab regimes, namely oil-producing countries in the Arab peninsula. There were also those who had alliances with the Pan-Arab Baath parties in Iraq and Syria. All those groups' leaders were members of the Fatah Revolutionary Council, which is equivalent to a party parliament. They argued, sometimes harshly, during meetings of that council. However, the balance of power was heavily tilted toward Arafat and his alliance, which included two of the main Fatah founders, Khalil Wazir and Salah Khalaf. Wazir was assassinated later in Tunisia by Israeli commandos. Khalaf was assassinated by a member of the Abu Nidal splinter group. The three leaders kept the balance of Fatah unity for as long as they could. They showed some support and sympathy to the smaller leftist and rightist groups when needed to keep them within the ranks.

Meeting Amjad in Sacramento started with cautious statements and slowly moved into political positions. Amjad showed me his understanding of my noncompromising beliefs. I found him to be intelligent, and somehow we found common goals. I left with good feelings. We agreed that we would go back to San Diego and start rallying the Palestinian and Arab students in support of the Palestinian cause as viewed by Fatah. We also agreed to start public relations and public awareness activities among the general American public and the different potentially supportive American groups and organizations including minorities. My journey with Fatah in America started right after that Sacramento meeting, however, timidly, I must say.

In San Diego, I gathered a few students who seemed like serious Palestinian patriots who wanted to do something for their people's cause. They all were Fatah supporters. The most active amongst them was a student named Mahmoud, who had dark black hair, a receding hairline, a round face, and a thick dark black mustache. He was quiet and did not talk much, but he was more committed than any of us. Even though I only knew him a short time before, I felt comfortable enough that we met often, although, mentally, I was not fully committed to Fatah supportive activities.

PSA Flight 182

About 2 months later, a large Palestinian American community convention took place in Albuquerque, New Mexico. I did not want to hassle with the trip, especially since it was by car and I was not over my road trip yet to San Diego from Texas. Mahmoud was accompanied by Ramez, a young Palestinian student who I did not personally know but who went on that trip. When it was time to come back, they took a flight to San Diego on Pacific Southwest Airlines. While over the city of San Diego approaching the airport runway, the plane collided with a smaller private plane, and both planes crashed to the ground in a residential neighborhood. All passengers and some residents were killed. All of San Diego was tense and sad over the horrible accident, especially since the airport was located right adjacent to downtown and was surrounded by high-rise buildings and thousands of homes. I had no idea the two guys were on that flight. I was expecting them to return by vehicles to Los Angeles.

That day, I received a phone call from Saber, the regional coordinator in Sacramento. He apparently was involved in the flight arrangement for the guys on the ill-fated plane. He said, "Mahmoud is dead; my condolences."

I said, "What are you talking about? How?"

He then told me that he was along with Ramez on the PSA flight. I asked if he was certain. He answered he was, very much so. Suddenly, death was following me again, all the way from Beirut. Mahmoud was dead because he went to that convention. I felt sad for the loss of his life. I thought I could have easily been with him on that flight. It was only fate that I chose not to go for any particular reason other than the discomfort and exhaustion of traveling by car.

Martyrs die in battles fighting for a cause they believe is worth their lives and the lives of many others. Although Mahmoud did not die in a battle, I still believed he was a martyr for Palestine. His death greatly affected me. I felt morally obligated to continue with what we both started. Both Muhannad and I encouraged him to take the lead. Muhannad was getting ready to graduate and leave for work in one of the Arab Gulf states, and I was trying to be a good student, so we both took a backseat. I felt if I did not take charge, I was letting Mahmoud down, and he would have died in vain. Subsequently, I became devoted to Palestinian activities throughout the United States.

Our Palestinian and Arab followers and supporters were growing size. We started out with a social-cultural club, which organized lectures on the Palestinian cause, invited speakers, activists, professors, and writers who were advocates of Palestinian rights. We also set up information desks on most American campuses and invited American university students to English-narrated documentaries which explained the story of our people. At first, very few American students showed interest in knowing more. However, as we began to look more familiar around campuses, their numbers grew significantly. We frequently conducted educational activities about the Palestinian cause.

Activities among Palestinian and Arab students were more argumentative due to the wide range of Arab students of different interests. Many of them were opposed to oppressive regimes in their own countries, and the Palestinian issue was lost in a mix of these issues. This was the case across all campuses in the U.S.

As Fatah supporters met from all regions of the U.S., we shared and discussed an alternative to the organization of Arab students which dominated most of the social, public relations, and political activities in the U.S. We believed the Palestine cause needed a focused student organization dedicated to it. A heated debate took place between advocates of the idea and those who opposed it, based on the belief that Palestine is part of the Arab nation. They believed we should have been a factor of Arab unity, not a divisive one. It was a valid opinion, but, we felt like a tiger in a cage. Our cause was a priority, we just did not want to waste effort and time entangled in Arab issues, which was the case of the OAS. I was one of the believers and advocates of an exclusive Palestinian student organization.

We won the debate, and we started the work to establish the General Union of Palestinian Students (GUPS); after all, it was an organization which existed since the sixties, had branches throughout the world, with its central body having representation in the Palestine National Council of the PLO representing Palestinian students in Palestine and the Diaspora. It was a logical choice. Seven of us from the east, west, south, north, and central United States regions, chosen by the leadership, got together. I was their general secretary. I was overwhelmed with the level of support and eagerness of Palestinian students to establish GUPS. My phone was ringing off the hook. Phone calls came from almost every significant city and town in the U.S. and most states. We sent out membership forms and received back thousands of applications. We held elections for local executive committees of all the branches and representatives to a national convention.

A couple of months later, in the summer of 1980, we held our convention. At least 3,000 people showed up in northwestern Illinois. It was a huge and emotional event. We were able to have supporters of Fatah and other Palestinian factions join forces in a great show of unity despite all our differences. The convention hall was full of students and community members. At the end when the names of the elected national executive committee were announced, I was named general secretary. All the committee stood on the stage facing thousands of people who clapped and chanted for few minutes: "We redeem Palestine with our blood and soul!"

GUPS had 72 branches, each in a different city, some cities had five to 10 different universities and community colleges, which were covered by one branch. Our student members were full of energy and wanted to give all they could to help. We set up informational desks and tables with many English books about Palestine, held forums and debates, and documentary movies were sent by carrier from city to city, on a daily basis. We often lost track of who had them at any particular time. The person who received them knew where to send them right after his event was concluded. We held many rallies and demonstrations on campuses and cities downtown. We had significant local media and sometimes national coverage. Zionist and pro-Israeli organizations tried to offset our activities, however, they could not keep up with us. We had the passion and the stamina to keep going every single day.

The years 1979 through 1982 were probably the most active grassroot work of Palestinian students and the Palestinian American community throughout the U.S.A. I could not go one weekend without having to fly to another city on Friday and fly back Sunday, to deliver a lecture for Palestinian and Arab students, or to be a key participant in a debate which hosted one or two supporters of other Palestinian factions . . . to discuss political strategies of the PLO, analyze events, discuss what went wrong, and offer projections of the future. I was especially known for being a good and a tough debater, which made me popular among Fatah supporters in most cities. I was also the leader of all student supporters of Fatah. I enjoyed a great deal of respect and held a high status in the community. I tried to be a polarizer and made my opinions helpful to sort out internal differences. I was respected by all, including those who did not agree with me. I also earned that respect through the commitment and work I put into organizing and building the strength of our new organization.

And I was closely watched by the FBI, although I was never directly approached by them. However, many of my friends and fellow activists who were questioned were asked many questions about me. Only one time did I receive a phone call from an FBI agent. He identified himself and sounded like Hikmat, a friend of mine. I thought it was a practical joke. My response was, "Yeah, OK, so go to hell," and I hung up the phone. I waited a few minutes. I thought Hikmat would call again, but he did not, so I proceeded to call him. I asked him what kind of a sick joke was he trying to pull on me. He swore that it was not him, and that he would never do such a thing. I thought he was being truthful. It was not part of his character to pull practical jokes. The agent never called again.

One other time a doctor friend and fellow activist in Los Angeles was paid a visit by the FBI at the hospital where he worked. At the cafeteria, the agent asked him if he knew me. My friend, as close as we were, only knew me by my nickname. He did not know my legal name which the FBI agent used, so my friend said that he did not know the person with the name he was asked about. The agent told him, "Doctor, don't deny that you know him. You were taped talking to him on the phone just last week, and several times before. Doctor, you may be involved in international terrorism without knowing it."

My friend, after this meeting, processed in his mind the last name they mentioned, and he asked that I meet him. When I met him, he told me about his meeting with the FBI. I was not surprised about their inquiry about me. I was, however, seriously concerned that they thought of me as a terrorist. I knew my noncompromising political views about Palestine were not accepted by the American government. I was against the idea of a two-state solution, which would return to the Palestinians 20 percent of historical Palestine, and denied the right of return to those who were ethnically cleansed out of their homes and cities, and to their descendants. I am one of them. Those were my political views, and I thought to myself since American people were free to like or dislike them, it was all within their freedom of speech protected by law. I never advocated any violence, but to the American government, armed struggle was considered terrorism, and anyone who supported it was a terrorist. I was referred to as terrorist or a "potential terrorist," as it seemed, at least internally within the FBI.

I was in the Middle East one summer. My flight back to the U.S. was through New York John Kennedy airport. Right at the entry point, the officer punched my name and read the screen and asked me to proceed to a nearby room; I did. I was sitting on a chair in that room when two immigration officers came and sat next to me. All other arrival passengers were gone by then. One of them was talking to the other and said, "What's with that Lebanese guy?" He was referring to me, because my American travel document stated my place of birth as Lebanon. The other officer answered, "Apparently he is a terrorist. They are running his papers now through the Bureau."

Just about when he finished these words, two officers came in the room with my travel documents. One of them looked at me and instructed me to follow him. The immigration officer who sat next me, said, with shock, "Is this the guy you were talking about?" I smiled, because I thought the formal Italian suit I was dressed in made him exclude me as someone who could be a terrorist suspect. I followed the officers out of the room. They asked me to open my luggage and started looking through everything that was in it. They asked me questions about my trip to the Middle East, and went on and on until I became aggravated and mad. They did not tell me the reason for stopping me. I got into an argument with one of them when he was examining my personal pictures. I said, "Since when do you look at pictures?"

He said, "Sir, we look at anything we want to look at."

I was angry and nervous and did not trust what they were up to. I heard stories about people with green cards like me at the time, who, at the airport, were denied entry and their green cards were cancelled. So I said, "OK, Officer, I want to say that I know my rights well, and I would like to call my attorney to be present."

The other officer who was much nicer said, "Where is your attorney?"

I said, "In Washington, D.C."

He said, "You want to bring your attorney from Washington?"

I said, "Yes, because you are not telling me why am I being stopped here. I will miss my connecting flight, and I don't know how long this will take."

The officer took me aside and said to me, "Please trust me, this will not take much longer. We know you are a leading activist in your community. It's presidential election season, and we are asked to be vigilant. I promise to personally escort you to your connecting airline once done, in few minutes."

I looked in his eyes and felt I could trust him. I said, "OK, I trust you." Sure enough, a few more minutes and they concluded the process. The officer escorted me, bypassed the crowd, and I made my connecting flight. The two officers who searched and questioned me did not leave me with much to think about, however the officer who sat next to me and stated that I was a terrorist did. I could never figure out why they thought of me as such. Was it for my political beliefs and opinions? It seemed that most activists who were viewed as extremists within the Palestinian American community were being monitored. Many others who were considered "moderates" were considered peace advocates and pro-American. They aspired to be accepted in the U.S. at both public and official levels. Those Palestinian Americans also tried very hard to

246

position themselves to play a bridging role between the PLO and the American government, a messenger role which earned many of them importance on both sides, the American and the Palestinian community, especially since, at the time, the American government did not recognize the PLO and had only a few major conditions for the PLO to meet before it could gain American recognition. With the PLO leadership eager to gain such recognition, those considered moderate Palestinian Americans became more active, and many of them competed with each other to reach out to American officials and introduced themselves as having direct contact with the PLO leadership, in particular, Yasser Arafat. American officials seemed to have directly or indirectly encouraged such a role. That way, they were talking to American citizens with a Palestinian background, which might influence Arafat to meet American conditions and become part of the Middle East peace process. Furthermore, a new American Palestinian organization was created called the "The Palestinian American Congress." It was meant to be an umbrella organization, to include all Palestinian American community organizations, societies, clubs, and unions as its members. Fatah supporters in the U.S. worked very hard to make that happen. We promoted the idea and advocated it as the right thing to do. The main idea was to create a lobbying voice in the U.S., a public relations body which could be legitimate, totally accepted, and most important, representative of the Palestinian American community.

We held a national convention in Washington, D.C., and elected a third-generation Palestinian American lawyer, the late Jawad George, for its president. Amjad, the U.S. Fatah supporter's general coordinator, soon after moved to Washington, a move which signified strategic interest on the part of Fatah and the PLO to be as close as possible to the official American government decision-making bodies and officials. The Palestinian American Congress was a very reassuring structure for the U.S. government that the Palestinian Americans are all under control and would not cause much trouble. Radical Palestinians also directed their activities within the congress. Despite the degree of anger with the American official foreign policy toward the Palestinian historical rights, the Palestinian activists in the U.S. never had any ill intention toward the American people or government. Almost all of us liked living in the U.S., adopted the American way of life, and had American friends, wives, or girlfriends. We liked America and its people. We just had a problem with American government blind support for Israel, while being against Palestinian rights to their homeland. We were denied our rights with an obvious double standard as compared to American international positions on human rights, democracy, freedom, and self-determination; which consecutive American governments supported in many parts of the world. We believed that when it came to Palestine, the rules changed. However, we never gave up on reaching out to the American people everywhere we could to tell our story.

Our student group of Fatah supporters in the U.S. consisted of both the dedicated and the dynamic; more important, we had great synergy and were able to support each other in the different regions of the U.S. Everyone was willing to travel, speak out, organize, or just participate in an important political event. I did not seek leadership of Fatah supporters in the U.S., but I found myself being nominated and elected, and I did not decline any nominations either. I became a leader of all Palestinian Fatah supporters in the U.S. through a group of seven activists. We planned, organized, and implemented hundreds of activities every year, to the point that our group became dominant and had a decisive weight on most Palestinian activities in the country. If we did not like what a well-known speaker had to say, we did not endorse him or sanction his lectures at all. It was important to us that an event speaker be someone who did not just advocate a two-state solution as a final settlement, he or she had to be clear on calling for the right of return of the pre-1948 Palestinians to their homes in their villages, towns, and cities. We put up with that grudgingly, and only as a transition to liberating all of Palestine.

Many Palestinian American community members and organizations did not agree with our political viewpoint. The community consisted of clubs which took names after towns its members originated from, like the Ramallah Federation, Beirah, Dir Dibwan, and many others. Those immigrants found themselves gathering in these clubs to help each other in the U.S., as well as support some development projects in their original hometowns in Palestine. Most of them were from the West Bank. Generally, all other Palestinian immigrants joined clubs, societies, organizations, and unions which had a more national Palestinian structure. However, those were smaller in numbers and more widely disbursed.

Palestinians from different countries of the Diaspora were fewer. Some were living in the same area, given that most Palestinian students or immigrants in general came to the U.S. with the help of a relative or a friend who immigrated before them. I wondered why the largest part of the Palestinian people, which is the refugees of 1948, were not represented in numbers reflective of their size. The PLO and Fatah representation structure was much more in favor of the West Bank Palestinians than any other. Gaza Palestinians were second in representation. Many PLO leaders used to point out that they themselves were from the pre-1948 areas of Palestine. While that was true, the bulk of the PLO body was far more governed by West Bank Palestinians than any other Palestinian segment. Most Palestinians did not like to address this issue directly. It was an underlying issue, and was discussed between middle- and lower-level activists within Fatah and the PLO from Lebanon, Syria, and other countries, not because of any resentment or envy but more because of fairness of representation. Such a structure certainly influenced the PLO political direction.

Chapter 11

Inside the PLO - Inflated and Confined in Lebanon

PLO compromises ended up in a famous proposition for a two-state solution, with a vague clause on the right of return of the pre-1948 refugees. Official statements were too flexible and meant to be interpreted to mean different things. The objective was to offer those refugees and their descendants the right to live almost anywhere they like, since the PLO leadership knew their original homeland was never seriously part of the agenda, except as a symbolic act. The Israeli government and many countries who supported Israel considered implementation of the right of return to mean the end of existence of the state of Israel based on the future change of demographics should the Palestinians return to their homeland. Palestinians' demographic distribution was never properly addressed within Palestinian internal politics. It was a taboo; the Palestinian National Council (PLC) was the Palestinian/PLO parliament in exile. It consisted of Palestinian representation from the different PLO factions and Palestinian communities throughout Palestine, the Arab countries, and the world. The only Palestinians who were not represented were those living in Israel, as Israeli citizens. Any association with the PLO was considered an act of treason to the state of Israel.

Members of the PLC were never chosen by direct elections. Elections were impossible. Palestinian refugees were living under the sovereignty of other governments which objected to their conducting elections; it was even much more difficult for Palestinians living in other countries. While some of those reasons were true, the leadership discovered them to be a good tool for continued control. PLO factions sanctioned quotas agreed upon between them based on their supporter numbers. Even unions and society organizations' members of the PLC were chosen by the leadership. The choice made support for decisions and political direction of the leadership almost guaranteed. Even the classified "independent members" were never truly independent of faction affiliation. They were chosen by agreement of the PLO faction leaders, even though the independents were not public supporters of one faction or the other. The PLO executive committee and the PLC structure were a reflection of how the factions' own internal elections were conducted.

Selection of representative members to their own general assembly conventions were directly influenced by the traditional leadership. Their reelection was guaranteed. It was a lifetime job. It was almost impossible for new leadership generations to rise. Potential leaders had to wait for someone to die in order for a new rising star to make it into the leadership committees. Such a style was a common practice for parties in the third world during the cold war era. They followed the model of the Soviet and Chinese communist parties. The only alternative was internal upheavals and differences between centers of powers within those parties which led to a coup, labeled as a corrective movement. This amounted to an overthrow of an existing leadership normally due a significant failure or defeat which leads to a loss of most of the party base. Otherwise, traditional leaders held their positions for decades and were praised and portrayed as superhumans with leadership gifts which were impossible to replace. That went on as long as that particular leader was alive. When a new leader rose to power, he was praised for his great and supertalents as well—most of the time by the same followers, who are actually very talented in shifting loyalties at a moment's notice.

The Palestinian revolution regime was very similar in that regard, except for the fact that many leaders were assassinated by the Israeli Secret Service. Some sacrificed their lives and sometimes their families' lives, and left behind very young kids who grew up with a haunting memory of the day an Israeli assassination Special Force stormed their homes and showered their father with bullets, leaving them screaming and crying over their parents' lifeless bodies. Some of those leaders died in their thirties or early forties. Others survived an explosion of a mailed package sent to them by the Israeli Secret Service or shots fired into hotels or in cafés in Europe. Those had to live with disfigurements or handicaps from the attacks. Some of the leaders who survived lived through their seventies and were still leaders of Fatah and other factions of the PLO in first and second rank leadership positions for more than 45 years.

Fatah supporters in the U.S. were able to be a unifying and a leading force. We knew how to attract leaders of all the different community groups. The PLO was viewed by Palestinians as their government. Frequent visits to Lebanon were made by leaders of the Palestinian American community. They met Yasser Arafat, Khalil al-Wazir, and other leaders. Many PLO leaders also came to the U.S., especially New York, the home of the United Nations. They joined meetings of the General Assembly or were observed at important meetings of the U.N Security Council. Most times, they stayed at the United Nations Plaza Hotel.

Faruq al-Qaddumi was one of the founders of Fatah and the PLO secretary of foreign affairs, equivalent to being a foreign minister of state. For over 30 years, Qaddumi held that title. He met with leaders and foreign ministers of the greatest countries of the world, amongst them, Brezhnev of the Soviet Union, China's great leader Mao Tse Tung, and Vietnam's legendary general Giáp. Many PLO representative offices were opened in these countries, and a good number of them were upgraded to embassy levels. The PLO was surely penetrating the world of diplomacy. We Palestinians were very happy to see the world recognizing our presence as a people. We felt progress toward regaining our right to our homeland. However, when years passed, I witnessed simple and humble revolutionaries, including those who adopted Marxist beliefs, become very similar to the Western type of diplomats, not just in their apparel, but also their lifestyles. Not exactly in harmony with the struggling refugees or people under occupation they represented! The wider base of Palestinians did not believe that such diplomatic-type of behavior really reflected their state of misery. A joke was often whispered among us, about our long-term serving ambassadors. The punch line of it was that most PLO ambassadors got confused and became representatives of *different* countries, and *not* the PLO. That was due to how much some of those ambassadors advocated the politics and interests of the countries they were stationed in. They held the seniority title of service amongst all Arab ambassadors. The embassy became their very own private business. They made good personal use of their diplomatic status. Very few PLO representatives were respected by the Palestinian community. But there were some who served the Palestinian cause with great dedication, and a number of these were assassinated in Europe by the Israeli intelligence, Mossad. Israel did not mind the corrupt Palestinian officials, but it was certain the effective ones were hated.

Between the years of 1978 to the middle of 1982, the Palestinian student movement in the U.S. had reached its peak of organization and activities. We were a vanguard to the Palestinian American community, as well as to the Arab American community. We believed in our cause and struggle that was led by the PLO *as a whole*, yet we felt that most of the top PLO leadership was leading us to political disaster. Their failure in Lebanon and the countries which hosted the largest populations of Palestinians was beyond any doubt. Namely, Lebanon, Syria, Jordan, Egypt, and to a lesser degree, Iraq. Military confrontations with the IDF from the South of Lebanon was proving to be at a great cost to the Palestinian revolution. Most Lebanese did not want to be the only Arabs to pay a heavy price for the Palestinian struggle while Palestinian revolutionary activities were minimal to insignificant in most other countries, including the West Bank and Gaza. PLO activities were totally disconnected from the Palestinians in pre-1948 Palestine.

To compensate for its weakness, the PLO continued the path of what was called "compromise." They accepted one political initiative after another, and none of them impressed Israeli leaders. There was no promising progress. Leftist factions, referred to as radical factions, showed more and more frustration with the PLO leadership. They intensified their military clashes and infiltrations against the IDF. That proved to be more and more difficult. The Southern Lebanese Army, the IDF arm in south Lebanon, created a zone which was well guarded. To infiltrate into territories of historic Palestine became almost impossible through land or sea.

Some factions got more creative by using flying gliders. They sent a few suicide fighters. If they succeeded in flying over the security zone without being discovered, they clashed with the IDF, and they had no way of making it back to their base. They either were killed in battle or captured by the IDF. Those who were killed were buried in what was, and still is, known as the "Cemeteries of Numbers." As previously mentioned, these are Israeli cemeteries where all Palestinian fighters were buried with a number tag on each tomb in lieu of a name to identify the dead. Even if the IDF knew who the dead Palestinian was, they still used a number and kept his record.

The PLO was cramped in Lebanon. It was the only solid base which was housing the PLO leadership and most of its infrastructure, military, financial, political, and informational. Menachem Begin, prime minister of Israel at the time, and Ariel Sharon, defense minister, both saw a great chance to devastate the PLO with a blow which would shatter its base and push away the threat of Palestinian armed struggle for decades. If the PLO lost Lebanon, it would not be able to substitute it.

Chapter 12

Invasion, Evacuation, Abandonment, and Massacres

1982 Israel Invasion of Lebanon

On June 3, 1982, an assassination attempt occurred on the life of the Israeli ambassador to the United Kingdom. The operation was carried out by the Fatah Revolutionary Council, a small splinter group led by Abu Nidal. He was a Fatah Revolutionary Council member. He was also the Fatah-appointed leader of the organization's branch in Iraq. Abu Nidal revolted against Arafat's leadership. He claimed Arafat and his leadership sold out Palestine. However, Abu Nidal himself was not so independent. He had support and access to the Iraqi intelligence network around the world. He carried out many attacks on embassies, airports, as well as on PLO representatives. Abu Nidal's group accused many PLO leaders of having shady contacts with Israelis. Abu Nidal's group operations were very questionable. The group appeared to be like a loose cannon. Later, the Iraqi intelligence used the group for its own agenda. The same thing happened with Muammar al-Gaddafi's regime in Libya, which also hosted Abu Nidal's group. It seemed to be doing favors for many intelligence services. One of the books written about the group was titled *A Gun for Hire*. That's fairly self-explanatory.

Despite the fact that the PLO was not responsible for the London assassination attempt, Menachem Begin and Ariel Sharon decided it was a good enough trigger to carry out an invasion of Lebanon. They called it "Operation Peace for Galilee." At first, it was thought to be a partial invasion, aimed at creating a buffer zone to prevent PLO fighters from having bases in all of South Lebanon, thereby securing Galilee from rockets and infiltrating Palestinian fighters. However, it was later discovered that Sharon intended to go all the way into Beirut. The ultimate goal was to uproot the PLO leadership headquarters and kick them out of Lebanon altogether.

The IDF pushed its way from the south in massive numbers of tanks and soldiers, circled one town after another where Palestinian fighters were based, and made sure supply lines from Beirut were cut off. The Palestinians fought bravely in many locations. To preserve their military presence,

262

Arafat's leadership ordered many of Fatah battalions to withdraw and be stationed in the Bekaa Valley in the east of Lebanon. It was obvious Palestinian fighting forces would not halt the IDF's overwhelming advance even though the Palestinian units which stayed in their positions fought to death—literally—in places like the Shaqif Castle (Beaufort or Belfort *Castle*), in Tyre, Sidon, and around Beirut. At the end, all those locations fell under the control of the invading army.

At least two Palestinian high-ranking military commanders stayed behind enemy lines with their men. They fought and were killed in battle. One of them was known as Bilal al-Awsat, and the other was Azmi Alzgayar. Both were missing in action for a long time. People who last saw Bilal, including local area witnesses, claimed they were sure he died fighting, although his body was never found. Azmi's body was never recovered either by the Palestinians, although it was taken to Israel. While alive, he had a long, unsettled account with Israel. Back on March 4, 1975, a group of eight fighters of Azmi's men, including a young woman named Dalal Al Mughrabi, who became an icon of the Palestinian struggle, carried out an attack in the north of Tel Aviv. It became known as the Savoy Hotel attack. They came by two rubber boats from

Lebanon, onto the shore, walked to the north-south road, formed a checkpoint, captured a bus of Israeli soldiers, took them, and headed to the Savoy Hotel. That attack was considered by Fatah as retaliation for the Israeli assassination of the three top-level PLO leaders in the heart of Beirut. The attack in Tel Aviv was deadly. All attackers except one were killed, and many Israelis were killed, including an Israeli commander. Azmi's body was, most likely, buried in the "Cemeteries of Numbers." Israel's government refused to return it, even though many prisoner and body exchanges took place several times since then.

In the south of Lebanon, hundreds of Palestinian fighters were killed, and thousands were taken prisoners by the IDF. The young fighters known as Ashbal (teenage fighters) inflicted large numbers of casualties amongst the IDF soldiers and destroyed many tanks. Soldiers of the IDF called them "The RPG kids." Many small groups fought on their own. They had no communication with their leadership, and certainly had no supply of food or arms. Most important, they had no hospital to send their wounded, so many of them bled to death on the battlegrounds. The Israeli air force bombed them with no mercy or concern for the civilian population. Multiple-story buildings, some 10 or more stories high, were bombed with vacuum bombs, which collapsed down to the ground. The IDF justification was that they were, at one point or another, occupied by Palestinian leaders or fighters.

Beirut under Siege

IDF tanks rolled to the Beirut outskirts from the south and east with complete coordination with the Lebanese Christian right militias. The IDF passed through and took positions easily in mountain hills overlooking West Beirut. Heavy artillery, surveillance equipment, and supply bases were established in the Christian right enclave. The north of Beirut was also controlled by Christian right-wing forces. The sea, to the west, was controlled by the Israeli navy, including destroyers with heavy artillery. Beirut was totally under siege. The air force continued to bomb around the clock and made life a living hell for the people of West Beirut. Yasser Arafat, his deputies, and all the top leaders of Fatah and other factions lived in cars or slept in basements of buildings they chose randomly. They would just park their cars and stay there. They walked between rubble and stopped to chat with their fighters. They boosted moral by talking about steadfastness and turning Beirut into another Stalingrad, the famous city which reversed the

Russian defeat by Hitler's forces into a victory. However, they knew reality on the ground, and knew that no real ally on the outside was providing help.

Palestinians fought alongside Lebanese National Movement fighters, who remained genuinely supportive of their Palestinian allies to the end. The Syrian army in the mountains and southeastern part of Lebanon put up a fight and lost many men by air bombing and ground engagement. The Syrian air force suffered a major defeat and lost 70 fighter jets in a couple of days. That was a blow to Hafez al-Assad's leadership and a blunt message that Syria would have been badly defeated if it came to the defense of the PLO. Palestinian and Lebanese fighters realized they were alone in that fight against a far superior power. The choice was either fight to the death or try to reach a war-ending agreement.

The United States sent Philip Habib, a Lebanese American, as an envoy to negotiate an agreement. The PLO leadership wanted an honorable end which would not show a surrender or a humiliating defeat by the Israelis. Mr. Obaidi was Arafat's media spokesman. He stressed in many news conferences that the PLO was only leaving Beirut if it was heading to Jerusalem. He and many Palestinian leaders, fighters, and activists believed Beirut was going to hold against the IDF and force it to retreat south. In later years, I got to know Mr. Obaidi and we met as friends in Ramallah. He once told me that during the siege of Beirut, he was with Arafat and with the presence of two other Fatah leaders, the late Mr. Hani al-Hasan, Arafat's political advisor, and General Saad Sayel, the PLO chief of staff. Arafat was having breakfast. The leaders discussed Philip Habib's proposal of PLO evacuation. After the meeting, Obaidi asked Arafat a direct and bold question: "Are we really going to leave Lebanon and evacuate?" Arafat replied, "Of course we are, what else can we do?" a disappointed Obaidi turned and walked out, a move which showed disrespect to Arafat and soured his relationship with Arafat and drove him out of Arafat's inner daily circle.

Watching IDF surround Beirut gave me the bitter feeling of humiliation. All my friends and comrades felt the same way. It was my last semester before I earned a bachelor's degree in civil engineering, and it was my last final exam when Beirut experienced the worst night of air bombing and artillery shelling ever. Thousands of bombs exploded everywhere to convince the Palestinian leaders they had no chance to hold their grounds. The next morning, instead of taking that final exam, I told my professor that I felt my head was about to explode and asked if he would postpone the exam a couple of days due to my worries about my family, friends, and people in Beirut. I had the highest grade in the class, so he agreed, I reached my family by phone and learned everyone was fine. A couple of days later, I took my exam and did well. I was very sad during my graduation which was held a few days later as the war was still raging. I could not celebrate and be happy.

Many student Fatah supporters in the U.S. were angry and feeling helpless. Many wanted to go to Lebanon and join their people in that fight. Many called me asking if I could arrange for them to travel. I made my calls to determine if there was a need for them. The answer from Beirut was no, they had no shortage of experienced fighters and didn't really need volunteers who might become a burden to be accommodated and trained during a very intense battle, so we relayed the message and calmed our supporters.

An agreement was reached: The PLO had to evacuate all its headquarters. Leadership, personnel, and all fighters must be out of Lebanon. They left for several countries; some traveled by land to Syria, most traveled by ships to Tunisia, Yemen, Sudan, and other countries. The deal was that fighters were allowed to carry their light weapons, similar to the AK-47 Kalashnikov. Ceremonies of voluntary evacuation of fighting positions were conducted, mainly symbolic acts, to show the Palestinians and the world that their fighters were not defeated and did not surrender. Nonetheless, the feeling was that of deep sadness and defeat, despite the well carried out show of pride by Arafat and the fighters themselves. They put up a good fight, sacrificed, and defended their revolution.

The day Arafat went on the boat, all national Lebanese leaders lined up to salute him. Bullets were fired in the air in a scene combined of pride and sadness. Fighters left their wives and children behind. Front pages of newspapers showed photographs of their historical departure. One newspaper showed a woman kissing her fighter husband's feet while he was on a departing truck, an expression of adoring love.

PLO Leaving Beirut, a Sad Moment of Truth

In America, my group and I watched with disbelief. Our dream was shattered! The revolution we once believed was undefeatable just lost its last base. No more armed struggle, and the future looked bleak, at best. We admired those who fought hard, and we felt very angry with the ones who just pulled out of the fight. We thought the revolution should have been much better prepared to remain steadfast and defeat the invaders. We were caught by shock. We grew much more resentful toward Fatah's leadership and the PLO leadership altogether. I lived most of the time in front of a television watching CNN. I was devastated and felt a new nightmare had just begun for our people. All the young men who sacrificed their lives, all those civilians who were killed, injured, homes and communities destroyed—did not pay off. A defeat came upon us, and certainly looked like it was pushing the Palestinian cause into a dark deep valley of death and loss.

IDF Storms Beirut

Right after the Palestinian fighters left Beirut, the IDF did not honor their end of the agreement to not invade Beirut. The Israelis claimed there were still fighters in Beirut, who the IDF needed to capture. They went into most neighborhoods, searched any building where Palestinians lived or hid. Many times, they captured whatever Palestinian man they found and took him to an unknown destination. My older brother Samih, along with my mother and younger sister Salma, were hiding in West Beirut. Samih escaped being captured on a few occasions. The IDF came into that building, searched, and left, while Samih was hiding. Matters were made much worse when Lebanese Christian right-wing militias painted their trucks to look like Lebanese army units, then went into West Beirut, searched for Palestinian men, captured hundreds, took them away, and they were never seen again. Very few European news agencies believed those men were executed and buried in mass graves in the Christian right-wing controlled enclaves in the mountains. Fakhri, my childhood friend and comrade, survived the civil war and the war with the IDF. He did not leave with the Palestinian fighters. He did not want to leave his family behind in the Shatila refugee camp while he escaped. Instead, he hid in different homes of Lebanese friends and supporters. Luckily, he was not captured.

As Fatah and the PLO factions were busy setting up their new offices and bases in different countries far away from the borders of Palestine, Lebanon's political structure was undergoing changes as well. It was time for the Lebanese Christian right-wing factions to make their gains. Bachir Gemayel, Israel's ally, became the only serious presidential candidate. He was quick to find admirers amongst most religious sectors of Lebanon, those who were ambitious to ride the wave of change. However, mainstream Lebanese of West Beirut and all other cities which were bases of support for the Lebanese National Movement and Palestinian factions were angry and felt totally humiliated. Preparations for armed resistance started to take place.

August 23, 1982, was the day Bachir Gemayel became the president-elect. His iron-fist rule was anticipated. A peace treaty with Israel was already drafted; in fact, according to many, Israel wanted Bachir to sign the peace treaty and begin normalization of relations before he even took office, but he played a little hard to get with Menachem Begin who grew very agitated and angry with him. Bachir needed to be in office first and control all of 10,452 square kilometers as he used to say. Bachir held many meetings with influential Lebanese and foreign dignitaries, and he wanted to make his office takeover as peaceful as possible.

Bachir Gemayel's Assassination

It was September 14, 1982. Bachir was meeting with a group of elite leaders of his party at one of the party's headquarters located in the East Beirut suburb of Ashrafiyeh when a huge explosion brought the building down. Bachir was found dead in the rubble. It was an event of great magnitude and a shock to those who liked him and those who hated him. No one knew what would happen afterward. To his foes, Bachir's presidency was bad news to come; the worst was expected. His death brought about a huge sigh of relief. He was known to be the most powerful and arrogant amongst the top Kataeb leaders. He also had a large support base in his community. Scenes of the explosion site— bodies of 26 other Kataeb leaders who were killed in the explosion—only served to fan the flames of the Christian right-wing faction and its allies. The IDF deployed more troops on the streets of Beirut. They claimed it wanted to restore order and avoid clashes between the Lebanese warring sides. They also circled Palestinian refugee camps in Beirut suburbs. The Palestinians of Lebanon knew big events were about to unfold as consequences of the assassination.

Sabra and Shatila Massacre

Many Palestinians who lived in the camps, or close to them, like my own family, and could hide somewhere in the middle of Lebanese communities did that. Most others stayed in their humble homes in the camps. Only a few young men stayed behind in the camps. The majority either left among the fighters or found a way to flee the country. The camps of Beirut during that time were mostly populated by women, children, and the elderly. They were promised safety as part of the agreement of the PLO evacuation. However, that did not happen in Shatila and Sabra refugee camps.

On September 16, 1982, and for 2 days after, a rampage of killings and raping was savagely conducted by Lebanese Christian right-wing forces. They were gathered on a hill overlooking Shatila, right next to the IDF forces, who were in the camps before. The IDF marked entrances and exits of the camps, including where the narrow walkways between the homes lead to. Many eyewitnesses, including some of the killers who participated, stated they had seen Elie Hobeika, intelligence chief of the Lebanese right-wing forces, to have been among the fighters. One said to have heard Hobeika say, "I don't want any Palestinian to come out of the camp alive." Hobeika's own bodyguard, Robert Hatem, code name "Cobra," authored a book titled *From Israel to Damascus,* published December 11, 2004, which was an exposé of Hobeika's rise to power and his devious, traitorous, criminal, and an overbearing lusty lifestyle. Cobra claims to have heard Hobeika tell his men he wanted "total extermination and the camp wiped out." Cobra also stated he overheard one of Hobeika's men in the camp during the massacre on radio communication telling Hobeika he had rounded up over 50 women and children and asked what to do with them. Hobeika answered, "This is the last time you ask me what to do! I told you what to do, you son of a bitch!"

Over 3,000 innocent women, children, and the elderly were brutally murdered. There were many stories of women who were raped, then their throats were slit. The IDF fired rounds of sky lighting shells during the massacre. News reached people in areas surrounding the camp. They figured something big was happening inside the camps. Eventually, reporters and Red Cross operatives went into the camp. Bodies were lying on the sides of the narrow walkways everywhere. People were shot, axed, or stabbed to death. A large number of Lebanese Shiites who lived on one side of the camp were also subjected to the same ugly acts of murder and horror. Many young men were rounded up and taken away.

Two news reporters went to the stadium located on the hill overlooking Shatila and saw many young male prisoners. Even though the stadium was an IDF base by then, these men were taken in trucks by Christian right-wing forces and were never seen again. Answering to how many Palestinians were killed by his forces in 1982, Fadi Frem, a top military leader of the Christian right-wing Lebanese forces at the time, said "You will have to wait until we dig for a subway."

Fakhri, my childhood friend and comrade, came out of his hiding after he heard the news. His immediate family was fortunate to have had been out of the camp. However, many distant relatives and neighbors he knew all his life were not so lucky. He went in and saw the victims firsthand. Some of the scenes were worse than a horror movie. This was real, especially what these criminals did to women and little girls before killing them. A few survived by lying between corpses and pretending to be dead. They heard the killers shouting, "If anyone is injured, we will take you to a hospital," then when an injured person tried to get up or moan in pain, he or she was shot in the head and finished off.

An Israeli investigation commission found Ariel Sharon indirectly responsible for the massacre. It cost him a few years away from public life before he went back and became prime minister. As for Elie Hobeika, he had a much worse fate. After changing alliances from Israel to Syria, he was appointed minister in one or two of the Lebanese governments. Eventually, he was named in an international lawsuit for the massacres. He vowed he was going to be a witness and tell everything he knew. He never made it. He was killed in a bomb explosion of a car parked on the roadside when his Range Rover passed by. No one claimed responsibility for killing him.

Palestinian Fighters Leaving Beirut 1982

Chapter 13

Everything Changed after the PLO Evacuation

I was one of the many who felt broken and defeated by the outcome of the 1982 Israeli invasion of Lebanon. But most of all, I was angry. I became bitter and resentful of the old guard leadership of Fatah and the PLO. They went on as usual, tried to show their shortcomings as a good example of being steadfast, and tried to make their greatest defeat as a great victory. Fatah, as an organization, had mastered the making of propaganda among the Palestinians everywhere. *Tabreer,* Arabic for "justification," was a powerful tool the leadership used to convince its cadres and popular supporters of what they wanted them to believe. They claimed the loss was not a big deal, that the revolution and Fatah were going to emerge stronger than ever. Arafat himself was known for his own media stunts. He captured the attention of major world media when he left on a ship from Beirut as he agreed to do at the end of the war. He did not declare his destination, leaving observers from around the world, including his own people, wondering where the leader disappeared. He showed up after a few days in Greece instead of going to any Arab country. Heading to Greece was Arafat's way of sending a message: he was angry at the Arab regimes' lack of support.

A few months later, on the first of January, Fatah celebrated its founding anniversary, which was also proclaimed as the anniversary of the launch of the current Palestinian revolution. The event took place in the pro-Soviet socialist republic of south Yemen. Fatah leaders organized the biggest celebration event they could put together. It was supposed to be a show of defiance and assurance that the PLO is still around and active. For the cadres, *Tabreer,* or "justification," was an understatement by then. Our group in the U.S. totally gave up on the leadership. We just wanted to see a major restructuring.

Farouq al-Qaddumi, one of the top Fatah leaders as well as foreign minister of the PLO, was a frequent visitor of New York, home of the United Nations. Our group used to gather in New York and meet with him at the United Nations Plaza Hotel where he used to stay. It was the first time we met him after the Israeli invasion of Lebanon, and after the Sabra and Shatila massacres. We were boiling with anger and wanted to hear what Fatah had for a strategy to continue an effective struggle after the great loss of its main base, Lebanon.

Mr. Qaddumi was known for his satiric sense of humor. He did not realize that Fatah supporters were not really interested in his usual humor, given the magnitude of the setback and the numbers of people killed just a few months before. I was hoping to see him show some sadness and responsibility. Instead, we heard preaching of how the leadership has it all under control. He told us some stories of his heroic stances during the past meetings of the Arab League's foreign ministers, and then in answer to my question about the leadership's new strategy, he delivered a lesson to me on the definition of what is "tactical" and what is "strategical," and went on to say that "all these new bases we gained in those countries, like Tunis, Sudan, Yemen . . . etc., constitute an accomplishment we must protect, because, for example, if we wanted to attack Israel from the Red Sea, I am sure our brothers in Yemen will not object to that." I was speechless and so was the entire group in the meeting. When we left, we were all wondering whether those leaders have any sense of what Palestinians were going through, and how ridiculous they sound when they were trying to turn defeat under their leadership into a historic victory. All those bases Qaddumi talked about were more like asylum bases than anything else. They were completely under the control of the host governments, and for sure no military action against Israel or otherwise was allowed. If any weapons existed in them, they were very light weapons, for very limited use, mainly guarding of the premises and leaders.

The leadership was immersed in a world of politics. Throughout the years, Fatah's majority and leadership of the PLO was never seriously challenged. Discussions of compromises, on fundamental rights of the people of Palestine were conducted in closed rooms with the leaders, and acted on without being publicized. Fatah's organization Tanzim, which consisted of people well educated in revolutionary education, along with its supporters in the unions of workers, women, students, and professional unions of the PLO, were instructed to only adopt the leadership political moves. Political positions voted on were mostly those already dictated by the leadership. And most of the time, political compromises were prepared statements with a double meaning, with wiggle room left for Fatah cadres, operatives, and supporters to explain it to their communities . . . as they saw fit. A perfect example was calling the two-state solution as a "transitional program," implying that the PLO was not really giving up 78 percent of the historic land of Palestine, but rather, accepting a state of 22 percent as a step toward liberating all of Palestine. However, to the rest of the world, it meant the PLO was recognizing Israel forever. The leadership was never transparent with the people of Palestine about its true political intentions.

The ambiguity was presented as a successful maneuvering tactic. The reality was, it was merely a tactic to give the leadership room to defend itself against criticism of the popular base while engaging in negotiations with far less ambitious objectives. Fatah leadership told us that world influential players, like the Soviet Union, and some European states, needed the Palestinians to show "flexibility." Such arguments held well when the PLO leadership showed strength on the ground, when it had a strong military force, which the leadership claimed would not be defeated, one that could push the enemy back.

The late Hani al-Hasan was a senior political advisor of Yasser Arafat. He visited us in the U.S. in 1978. One time he came to our apartment where my close friend Muhannad and I were roommates.

We gathered at least 25 supporters to meet him and listen to what he had to say. He clearly stated, "The Palestinian fighting forces in Lebanon were then composed of small units, and when put together, constituted an army so flexible to fight a classical war, yet so capable of breaking up and fighting a 'guerrilla warfare,'" a definition of small numbers of units fighting without holding specific land. Units that can move around, hide, appear, and fight, then disappear. That was only for a short time, and it was only a few days before the IDF took control of all of South Lebanon, all the way to the borders of Beirut, and circled Beirut.

The PLO forced an exodus out of Beirut and the south of Lebanon, and the massacres were beyond the top leader's distinguished skills to justify and assure their support base in the future was going to be fine.

There I was in the U.S. after graduation. I couldn't go back to Lebanon and couldn't go anywhere. Without much choice, I decided to stay. I tried to get an entry job as a newly graduated civil engineer. It seemed harder than anything I had ever done before. The job market was very weak. I had more time on my hands, so I became more politically active. I traveled from one city to another giving political lectures to Palestinian students and community members. My obvious statements were those of unhappiness about the performance of the leadership, and that we expected accountability and new direction.

In the late spring of 1983, I went on a trip to Damascus along with Amjad, the head of Fatah supporters in the U.S. It was only the two of us on that trip. He had a relationship with Fatah leadership. We met up with Professor Naseer Aruri, who was a well-known intellectual. Most of the trip from Washington, D.C., to Paris, Aruri was talking, giving us his prospective and analysis on the Middle East political events. I had never seen Amjad so anxious to ask questions, listen to answers, and take so many notes. It was my first time on a trip to meet leaders.

Amjad was a smart man, politically savvy, and knew how to keep good relations with all leaders of Fatah. I found out later that Amjad needed the opinion of an intellectual like Aruri in order to speak impressively about the United States, policies, as well as the social, religious, and economic sectors of the American society,(which influenced the U.S. in its decision-making process.) The PLO leadership was very eager to get an entry into the U.S. political system and start a meaningful political relationship with the U.S. administration. They tried many avenues, such as organizations, individuals, former senators—anyone who claimed to have a relationship which might start some kind of a dialogue, even if it was a secretive process. The PLO also used all those different sources to find a way around the U.S. law which banned American officials from contacting PLO members as long as the PLO did not renounce terrorism and recognize Israel's right to exist.

Our meetings started right at the Damascus airport. By coincidence, we arrived at the same time that two of the founding leaders of Fatah were preparing to depart. One of them was Salah Khalaf. He was known to the media as the number-two leader after Arafat at the time. He was accompanied by Mahmoud Abbas, the man who became president of the Palestinian Authority and chairman of the PLO after Yasser Arafat. Abbas was not very popular within the Fatah supporter base.

Amjad and I walked right into the VIP room where both leaders were resting before boarding their plane to Tunis. It was my first time meeting the two leaders face-to-face. They were both joking. Salah Khalaf was teasing Mahmoud Abbas by turning to us and saying, "You guys need to hurry up and save me from this man before he turns me into an Israeli sympathizer." He did not mean that literally, yet he was indicating how much Mahmoud Abbas was making efforts with the old guard leadership of Fatah to understand the Israeli side. Abbas was known then to be the man of the compromising ideas. He was the first to advocate the two-state solution and a Palestinian-Jordanian confederate state. Abbas was never ambiguous about his beliefs.

Salah Khalaf asked me about my background, where I was born and raised, and wondered why I never met him during my long time in Beirut. It was a short, casual meeting and did not get into any deep discussion. However, Khalaf's remarks about Abbas were significant during that time, and gave me insight into some of the leadership's inner-circle discussions.

The first night upon arriving we met at Abu Fathi's home. He was Arafat's office manager, but he certainly was one of his critics as well. A group of second-tier leaders of Fatah was also present. Discussion started and was mostly about the shortcomings and ill performance of the leadership. Other groups within Fatah had formed inner circles, sort of cliques. They all held brainstorming meetings. The one big question, which was famous for being posed in the past by Vladimir Lenin, the famous founding leader of the Russian communist party and leader of the Bolshevik revolution against the czarist regime, was: "What is to be done?" which in Arabic meant *Ma al-amal?* The quote had an impact on most revolutionaries in the Arab countries, especially Palestinian and Lebanese communists and pro-Soviet socialists.

The next day, we had a meeting with Maher Ghunaim, one the old guard leadership and director of Fatah's Tanzim all over the world. Under him, he had a council of intellectuals and organizers who traveled from one country to another to maintain and strengthen Fatah's Tanzim and supporter groups. It was very customary for these leaders to start talking, and their guests to feel like they are in a political history lecture. I used to joke with my comrades by telling them when one of us visited a leader, "The guest will be very lucky if the leader starts his lecture from the era of the British mandate of Palestine." Some of them started from the early times of history, of course with a version which accommodated his analysis of current events, however, After leaving his office, I felt like we learned nothing to address the pathetic disarray of our cause and the fragmentation of our people.

In that afternoon, we had a meeting with Samih Quake, better known as Qadri. He was then a new-generation leader, his first time elected as member of Fatah's top leadership committee, the Central Committee. The man was full of anger and criticism. He was bold and mocking. In a way, I agreed with points he made but hated his presentation.

Amjad and I were coming out of Arafat's office once when we ran into Colonel Said Musa, known to most as "Abu Musa," a Fatah military general, with a reputation of a great fighter with an outstanding performance during the siege of Beirut. He had good character, fought in the south of Lebanon against the IDF, and scored many small victories. He also stood up to the Syrian forces and delivered a blow to their advancing armored battalions in the southern Lebanese city of Sidon. During that short street encounter, he told us that he had enough of Arafat's leadership. He was angry and frustrated. We promised to visit him as soon as we could.

Chapter 14

Fatah Split, Fatah Intifada, Last Hope of Change Dies

It was less than a week since Amjad and I had been in Damascus, and 2 days after our street encounter with Colonel Abu Musa that the news of mutiny broke out. It took a couple of days before the international media reported it. Colonel Abu Musa went to Lebanon's Bekaa Valley, where Fatah still had military bases. He stationed himself in the base closest to enemy lines, and the IDF was still occupying a good portion of Lebanon. From there, he declared mutiny. It was a quick reaction to contest a decree, announced 2 days prior, by which Arafat reshuffled the entire military leadership. To most members' disappointment, Arafat seemed to have strengthened those leaders with the worst performance in the last war with the IDF. He, at the same time, punished the ones who earned a hero's reputation, like Colonel Abu Musa, and his long-term friend and comrade and leadership critic, Abu Khalid al-Amleh.

At first the mutiny seemed like a small event, involving only one general and one base. It actually turned out to be a much-bigger movement planned and organized by two of the top leadership Central Committee members, four other generals, and a number of Tanzim leaders. It was the first serious threat to Fatah's unity, and its old guard leadership in the nearly 20 years of its founding. When names of the people involved were publicized, it was suddenly a Palestinian political earthquake. The event became the focus activity of all PLO factions.

Within a few days, it was obvious the Syrian regime granted logistical support to the mutiny. Differences between the Syrian president and Chairman Yasser Arafat had reached a zenith. A meeting between the two leaders had been held a couple of days before the mutiny. Amjad and I learned of its details during our visit to Samih Quake, Central Committee member and one of the main leaders of the mutiny. Abdel Muhsin Abu Maizer, PLO Central Committee member and the official spokesman of the PLO at the time, came in unannounced. He was one of Arafat's delegation to the meeting with President Assad. Samih Quake had a big smile on his face and said to Abu Maizer, "All right, now let us in on all the good stuff not published in the newspapers."

Abu Maizer then started telling what went on in the meeting with Assad. He mentioned that Arafat did not say a word in that meeting. He did not even comment on Assad's lengthy opening remarks, which seemed to include frustration mixed with mistrust of Arafat. According to Abu Maizer, President Assad was upset that whenever the PLO was approached by pro-U.S. Arab regimes to participate in a possible Middle East peace settlement, Palestinian propaganda was heightened about the need for its "independence of decision making," a slogan historically raised by the PLO against the Syrian regime to minimize its interference or attempt to control the PLO. Assad meant that the PLO intended to go it alone in reaching a settlement with Israel, leaving Syria isolated and in a much-weaker position to negotiate liberating its own Golan Heights from Israel, and the terms of potential permanent agreement.

Assad considered Sadat's peace treaty with Israel as capitulation of Egypt. In addition to weakening the Arab nation, he did not want something similar be slammed on him. He also thought Arafat was ready to abandon a collective Arab approach to peace with Israel in favor of a one-track, Palestinian-Israeli peace treaty. Assad was very bitter during that meeting, specifically about Arafat's nonrecognition of the Syrian army participation in the 1982 war. Assad said, "You deny our fighting role in the war. What do I say to all the mothers and wives of the men we lost in the war? How do I say they were killed?" That was a response to Arafat who repeated time and again in his speeches after the war that Palestinians were left alone to fight against Israel.

The PLO expected Syria to have a far bigger role in the fight than it actually did. The PLO and the Palestinians were totally disappointed. Syria, however, did not want to go into a full-scale war, especially since it had lost 70 warplanes and most of its air defense missiles systems in the east of Lebanon. They were bombed out and destroyed by the Israeli air force. Tens of tanks, trucks, and armored vehicles were destroyed, in addition to hundreds of soldiers who died. Those losses were enough to convince Assad the IDF was capable of reaching the gates of Damascus should he enter the war on the side of the Palestinians. He kept Syrian forces' engagement limited, just short of an all-out war.

After Assad's remarks to the PLO delegation, the PFLP faction represented by George Hasbash's deputy, Abu Maher al-Yamani, a very well respected Palestinian leader, suggested the delegations leave the Syrian president and Chairman Arafat together so they could have a private meeting. Neither Chairman Arafat nor President Assad seemed eager for that and both diplomatically avoided it. Small talk followed, and the meeting adjourned.

A few days later, right after the mutiny, Arafat made statements while in Damascus criticizing Syrian intervention in Palestinian affairs. The Syrian regime, in response, demanded he leave Syria on the next flight out, a move Arafat was quick to use as further evidence of Syrian regime animosity.

Anxious to know more about the magnitude of the unfolding Palestinian times ahead, Amjad and I decided to pay a visit to the defiant Colonel Abu Musa at the military base in eastern Lebanon. We arranged for a ride on a Jeep which drove through a road known as the Military Road, used only by the Syrian army and the Palestinian military factions, from Syria into Lebanon and vice versa. It was around 10 P.M. when we arrived at the entrance to the base. Abu Musa's men were alert, fully armed, and on guard for anyone or anything moving around them. At the checkpoint, the driver identified us as friends of the colonel, so the Jeep was signaled to pass through the checkpoint and onto the base. We were led into a small two-story building. Colonel Abu Musa was expecting us on the second floor. He knew Amjad very well but had only met me a couple of days earlier. I felt very honored to be in the command post of a well-known Palestinian hero.

Colonel Abu Musa was very welcoming. I joked around with him when I saw him struggling to light a small kerosene lamp, the type I remembered seeing in my childhood. I said, "Here you are causing all this commotion and only worrying about a kerosene lamp." He laughed hard. Then we had some tea while he told us about his motivation to start what he called "intifada," Arabic for "uprising" against the old guard leadership. He said, "They have deviated from the national liberation program of Fatah and the PLO, only to pursue a sellout agenda which will diminish the Palestinian armed struggle." He informed us of a list of demands he wanted the old guard Central Committee to adopt in order for him and his group to end the military uprising. Those demands were stated in an official statement by Abu Musa and the other four mutiny leaders. They demanded Yasser Arafat and his leadership:

1. cancel his military reshuffle decree.
2. hold a Fatah general convention to conduct accountability of those within Fatah who performed poorly during the war.
3. end corruption by many high-ranking officers and leaders.
4. adopt a clear political strategy with armed struggle being its cornerstone and an unquestionable approach until liberation is achieved.

Amjad and I concluded our visit to Abu Musa, wished him well, promised our solidarity with him and support for his demands, and headed back to Damascus. We arrived at our hotel in the early morning.

For the next few days, we were Abu Musa's advocates, albeit our close friends and comrades in Fatah were being much more cautious. They urged both of us to slow down on our zeal and wishful thinking that fundamental change was about to happen within Fatah. Our friends were much more experienced in Fatah's inner circles and knew that the uprising belonged to one clique which they didn't entirely agree with. Most of Fatah's small cliques disagreed with the old guard leadership, and at the same time, disagreed with each other. That fragmentation was the main cause of the inability to build a formidable opposition to Arafat and his leadership.

Fatah's leadership realized the seriousness of the military mutiny, which started on one base, and soon after, many other bases declared their support and loyalty to Abu Musa's command. More important was Syria's role, which limited Arafat's leadership of a military solution. Resorting to arms was unavoidable. Clashes started at checkpoints when each side took a prisoner or shot someone in a speeding car. Suddenly, comrades in arms for many years were now enemies, calling each other traitors, shooting and killing one another. It was my first time to witness how some of us Palestinians can be so mean and ruthless toward one another. I certainly witnessed different PLO factions clash with gunfire, even though we believed that Fatah represented the Palestinian national spirit. It was supposed to be kind and tolerant, especially when differences existed within the Fatah house. It seemed to me that the defeat in Lebanon and the massacres which followed filled many hearts with bitterness, blame, and anger. Now many could not accept moving forward without a major shakeup and accountability.

While in Damascus, Amjad and I visited the famous leader of the Popular Front for the Liberation of Palestine, the late George Habash. Dr. Habash was known for his honesty, integrity, and respect. Meeting him in such a close setting reinforced the good things I knew about him. He was sincere, realistic, and a very humble man. He was no longer that man who spoke with fired emotions. A couple of years earlier, he had suffered a stroke which left his right side partially paralyzed. His speech ability was back to normal, but his arm and leg functions were not. I was sad to see this historic Palestinian leader in that physical condition. The crux of his message to us was that we needed to be careful, and while revolting against Fatah leadership, not to fall in the grip of Arab regimes. He was insinuating the Syrian and Libyan regimes, as both were supporters of any move against Arafat's leadership. Habash also warned us against further splits within the Palestinian movement. The next day we met with his deputy, Mustafa al-Zibri, known as Abu Ali. He was very critical of the PLO direction. He also seemed to have a lot of energy to work within the opposition ranks of the PLO.

We went back to the U.S. where our comrades and supporters were anxiously anticipating our return. News of the internal turmoil was already out. We needed to decide on a new direction. Our Palestinian community became divided, and the student base of supporters and independents alike were engaged in debates and heated arguments on almost every campus. We met for long hours and many days, discussed, and evaluated. The general sentiment was very supportive of the new uprising movement. Even though we did not want to see a split within Fatah, we, for sure, wanted to see the old guard leadership come to grips with its shortcomings, implement serious reforms, and weed out the corrupt and overcompromising individuals. Fatah needed to live up to its original charter and reinforce its founding principal beliefs, which were the pillars of the modern Palestinian revolution launched in 1965.

We called for a convention for all Fatah leading supporters in the U.S. It was held in the summer of 1983 in Washington, D.C. It was customary for such conferences to elect Amjad as the chairman of the conference. Instead, however, and as a reflection of the heavy presence of our student group . . . and without my prior knowledge or expectations . . . in an unusual motion, they nominated me to be the chairman. The motion was quickly seconded by others, which put Amjad in an awkward position of not being nominated by anyone. A vote followed, and I was elected chairman of the conference. For the first time in many years, Amjad was undermined, and for the rest of the 2-day conference, he felt pushed aside. During a break he whispered to me, "Mr. Osama, is this what I have become—a single vote in the room?"

He thought I had orchestrated a soft coup to push him out. Only two people, one of them, Amjad, were asking the conference not to rush and declare siding with Abu Musa's uprising. Their voices were outnumbered; a clear decision was made and declared total support of the Fatah uprising.

Two days later, the old guard leadership learned of our new position. They were shocked about losing the support of the Palestinian American community and its student movement. It was a serious blow. The conference demanded that Amjad meet the uprising leaders, deliver our resolutions, and terminate our relationship with the old guard leadership. He did, although hesitantly, and from that point on, divisions among the Palestinian American community were initiated.

We organized numerous lectures in most cities and campuses to explain the demands of the Fatah cadres' uprising. At first we were met with cautious support. Some people were not opposed to our new direction, but kept silent. A few were very excited and showed great enthusiasm for the uprising to succeed. It was not too long before shooting clashes in East Lebanon contributed to doubts. No Palestinian activist or nationalist wanted to see Palestinians kill one another. The Fatah old guard leadership screamed everywhere, supported by the moderate Arab media and Western media. They all portrayed the uprising as a large-scale Syrian conspiracy to split Fatah and minimize its standing leadership of the PLO, an attempt to replace Arafat with a pro-Syrian Palestinian leadership.

The Battle of Tripoli

There was little doubt that Arafat's leadership possessed mastery of political tactics, more so within the Palestinian political movement and the Arab League. Fatah still had a strong presence in the major northern Lebanese city of Tripoli, a few miles from the Syrian border. It was mostly a Sunni Muslim community, which found in Arafat a godfather, financial supporter, and protector. It was a great environment for Arafat. He spent a lot of money fortifying Fatah's presence in Tripoli and sent fighters into the two refugee camps adjacent to the city, Baddawi and Nahr al-Bared. He found a great ally in a Muslim Sunni religious armed group called the "Al Tawheed movement" led by Sheikh Hasan Shaaban.

After preparing the grounds, Arafat's second in command, Khalil al-Wazir, who was well respected and known for his integrity and support of armed struggle, showed up in Tripoli. He organized and led Fatah's fighters and coordinated a strategy with Sheikh Shaaban. Shortly after, Arafat, himself, secretly rode a boat from Cyprus and landed in Tripoli. The showdown was underway; he had many media appearances and issued harsh statements against the Syrian-supported mutiny. He obviously planned to intimidate the Syrians and their Palestinian allies to start a military operation against Palestinian and Lebanese forces in Tripoli. He even went as far as providing support to the anti-Assad Muslim Brotherhood movement in Syria, which, if all else failed, was an almost guaranteed move to push Assad's regime to the limit. Arafat knew once a fight started, the result would show beyond doubt, to Palestinians everywhere—and the whole world—the mutiny called *uprising* was only a Syrian conspiracy. Events which followed proved it a success.

It was not long after that the Palestinian forces of Abu Musa, along with the Syrian-controlled Palestine Liberation Army units stationed in Syria, approached Tripoli from the north and east. The attack was led by former Fatah Colonel Abu Khalid al-Amleh, a man I got to know up close during that time. The battle was decisively in favor of the Syrian-supported uprising. Arafat had to evacuate again, that time on a French navy boat sent to escort him out of Tripoli. His departure was covered by world media. Watching the news from the U.S. compelled me and my group to go on a fact-finding mission. Palestinian infighting left a bitter taste in our mouths and cast doubts in our minds about the new uprising. Fatah unity seemed to have been lost forever. Soon, it was Amjad and I, again, leaving on another trip to Damascus. That trip gave me a different prospective. While visiting Fatah's uprising leaders, one at a time, I noticed how intrusive the Syrians were in the uprising and how much our new uprising became the mouthpieces of Syrian politics because they issued statements of blind support of Assad's regime.

Amjad and I went to Tripoli, met with the commander in the field, went into the camp and met a few people, then we visited Jameel's home in Nahr al-Bared refugee camp. Jameel was one of our student leaders in the U.S., the group which I led. He had moved back to Lebanon a few months before. I could tell he was not very happy with what he witnessed. He also had doubts. However, I was still in denial. I wanted to see that uprising as honest and genuine change initialed by independent Fatah leaders.

Nidal

During my stay in Damascus, I learned that Nidal, my good ol' friend and comrade from Beirut, was stationed there as well. I asked someone who was in contact with him to inform him of my presence and that I very much would like to see him. We met the next day at one of the uprising leaders' office. He had also joined the ranks of antileadership uprising. We only met for 2 hours, during which time I felt some distance between us. I thought Nidal saw me as a changed person, influenced by my living in America.

I was not ready to accept that distance, wars, and immigration can create changes between friends. For a few years I was not present in my friends' daily lives. True, I did not know what Nidal, Fakhri, and others had lived through, especially with the Israeli invasion. That was the last time I saw Nidal. A few months later, he moved to Bulgaria to study for a graduate degree. He had a relationship with a Bulgarian woman. I heard from friends I met later, who happened to have met him in Bulgaria, that he was generally depressed and continued to be sad over the dramatic changes of his life, added to the loss of his left arm and left eye and remaining scars. While on his way home one evening, he was attacked by a Bulgarian street gang. They beat him badly. He could not defend himself. After that, he sank deeper into depression, took too much medication, drank a lot of alcohol . . . and died of an overdose.

On my last day in Damascus, and on my way to the airport, one of the uprising administrators told me, "The Syrians want to see you." I was astonished and asked, "Why me?" He said it was standard procedure.

The driver who took me to the airport stopped in front of a high-rise building, and then asked me to get out of the car and go into the building. I said, "Who do I ask for?" He replied, "Just walk in and tell them who you are and they will take it from there."

I walked into the building, and for sure, they took it from there. I was led into a dungeon and into a room which looked like an interrogation room. It had an iron desk, iron chairs, and there was nothing else in the room. Three men walked in, handed me a long form which had so many questions about almost everything in my life: my name, addresses for the last several years, what I did for a living, my siblings, where they worked, where each lived—on and on. After I completed the form, the three men took turns asking me questions about our group in the U.S., our political affiliations, and who I met in Damascus. I answered their questions and told them I only met the top leaders of the Fatah uprising who were supposed to be their allies. I was hoping that would vouch for me being sympathetic to their regime. It was not the case. Instead, they asked, "What did these people tell you?"

I thought, *Wow, THESE PEOPLE!!!!* It was an expression used to belittle those Palestinian leaders of the pro-Syrian uprising. I was shocked at how little respect the Syrian intelligence had for them.

Those were the same leaders shown and talked about all over Syrian television stations and newspapers. Just 2 days before, they had a highly publicized meeting with President Assad! Broadcast commentators gave them more praises than they expected. I thought to myself, apparently what's on the news and propaganda was one thing and reality was something else altogether.

On my way to the U.S., I made a stop in London and visited with Fakhri, my childhood friend and comrade. He had moved to the UK after the Sabra and Shatila massacre, where he was studying the printing profession and had married. He told me about some of the horrible acts he witnessed the morning after the massacre when he went into the camp to check on his relatives.

Second Thoughts

Back in the U.S., I went on a tour again to different cities, where Palestinian students and Palestinian American community activists wanted to know where developments were leading. I hesitantly presented our fact-finding mission, as we saw it, which was an attempt by Arafat to discredit the new uprising. However, the reaction and satiric comments interrupting my lectures gave me a wake-up call. I found myself for the first time viewed as not being sincere, or, at best, as naïve, manipulated, and deceived. At one time during the lecture, I said, "You can consider me a witness," and that is when one of the attendees spoke out loudly, *"Shahed ma shafsh haga."* He quoted the title of a famous Egyptian play, *The Witness Who Did Not Really See Anything.* Then he continued, "Brother Osama, *you* are the witness who did not see anything." Everyone laughed, including me, but the comment struck me inside as true. That was my last lecture advocating the new uprising. I realized I made a big mistake.

Our group's activities were aimed at educating Palestinian and Arab American communities on political events and worked to promote the Palestinian cause among the American people. Instead of that, we became busy debating each other and fighting over control of existing community organizations, like the Palestine Congress of North America, the student union of Palestinian students, and many other organizations. Fatah supporters constituted the majority of their executive committees.

Fatah's old guard leadership sent many envoys to the U.S. They met with those who were not happy with our new adopted political line. They quickly hired the politically unemployed, those we thought of as opportunists and self-serving. We had voted them out in the recent past, and they were on forced retirement from being involved. Suddenly, they were active again. After all, Palestinian American and Arab American communities were significant in size, enabling these reinstated leaders to make a nice income through significant opportunities presented to them. It seemed that they considered the cause as "business opportunities" for their own personal benefit as they could be in constant contact with diplomats and leaders in the U.S. and the Middle East.

We went through most of the year 1983, all of 1984, and the first part of 1985 with nothing but accusations and counteraccusations. During that time, our support base shrank, as Syria's Assad and Libya's Gaddafi's influence on the Fatah uprising became more evident. Meanwhile, Amjad, our general coordinator in the U.S., saw a good opportunity of becoming one of the top leaders of the Fatah uprising. It was by then shaped as a new faction, rather than part of mainstream Fatah. Amjad moved with his family to Damascus. The uprising movement had a reshuffle of its own. First, it had pushed aside its chairman, Abu Saleh, despite him being a historic Fatah leader, replaced him by Samih Quake, and then Quake was pushed away in favor of Colonel Abu Musa. They lost the largest portion of their supporters.

In the U.S., our group slowed down its activities. Colonel Abu Khalid al-Amleh was the most powerful man within the uprising. I met him in Damascus several times, mostly at his home. I watched him become more and more of a dictator, who lived in his own world; he did not care what anyone else thought. He spoke passionately and liked a person . . . as long as that person agreed his him, even better if the person adopted and promoted his political viewpoint.

War of the Beirut Camps

The Shiite militia Amal, with Syria's support, became the main force in Beirut. It was also leading Lebanese resistance against the Israeli occupation of 1982. Amal was totally opposed to any armed Palestinian comeback into the camps. It even circled the camps and strangled the movement of

310

Palestinian arms and personnel. I came to learn from a friend years later that Abu Saleh, one of Fatah's uprising key leaders, took a trip from Damascus to the Beirut camps. It was in the second part of the year 1984, and he was accompanied by my friend. While in Beirut, Abu Saleh declared that Fatah will be back in the camps of Lebanon. And that caused him to be totally out of the Syrians' favor. I knew Abu Saleh, and met him many times in formal and relaxed meetings. He considered himself an independent Fatah founding leader and was proud of being an ally of the Soviet communist leadership and the Syrian regime. However, he insisted on his independence of any non-Palestinian influence, something the Syrian regime did not feel comfortable with. We used to have a saying which rhymed when spoken in Arabic. Translated, it meant "Syrian regime does not want allies, it only wants agents."

When Abu Saleh, accompanied by my friend, was back in Damascus, it was about 7 A.M. They walked into his office. A few minutes later the phone rang. On the other end of the phone was Abdul Halim Khaddam, Syria's vice president, and he was also Assad's man to manage Lebanon affairs. My friend could hear Khaddam screaming in Abu Saleh's ears, while Abu Saleh's face was turning red. He was very upset.

"Who told you to go to Beirut? How can you do that without our clearance? You guys think you can do anything you want in Lebanon? Don't ever do it again!" and he hung up. My friend noticed Abu Saleh's sinking expression. His end in Palestinian politics was decided right after that day. Abu Saleh retired to his home and died quietly a couple of years later of some sickness. He was a good man and a sincere Palestinian leader.

Amal Shiite Militia continued to agitate Palestinians at the camp's entrances, with daily intimidations and random assassinations at checkpoints. Amal then launched an all-out attack on Beirut Palestinian refugee camps in April 1985. It was a massive, vicious, and bitter attack. Palestinians fought bravely with minimal means. They made Amal pay a heavy price. Amal militia advanced in the Sabra neighborhood, where some of their fighters raped women, killed men for just being Palestinian, and robbed homes. Palestinians in the camps ran out of food. Ironically, some of the Amal militia acts, while claiming to be a liberating force and pro-Palestine, were similar to the massacres carried out by the Lebanese Christian right-wing forces. Syria's

Abdul Halim Khaddam was very supportive of Amal actions and was in favor of clearing the camps of all arms at any price of civilian lives. Fatah's uprising leader Abu Khalid al-Amleh's statements were just shy of blaming Amal and the Syrian regime support of its attack. Colonel Abu Musa was very outspoken that Syria must act to stop the bloodshed. We talked to him by phone. He was very critical of the Syrian regime despite his knowledge that his phone was most likely tapped by Syrian intelligence. However, he was sincere and lived up to his reputation. He told us that his forces in the mountains overlooking Beirut were not allowed by the Syrians to reload their guns because they used them to bomb Amal positions surrounding the camps in an attempt to stop the advance of Amal forces. In the end, it was the Soviet Union's ambassador to Damascus, and other diplomats, who played a major role in reaching a cease-fire and stop the bloody attack.

Fatah Uprising, a Hope Died

The war of the camps was the straw which broke the camel's back. Fatah's uprising leadership was the same as Arafat's, especially when it came to protecting and defending the lives of the people. The old leadership tolerated corruption, was weak, ill prepared, and did a poor job of planning. Fatah's uprising leadership did not take the right stand when the moment called for it. They could not resist Syrian pressure and influence. I was once talking by phone to one of Abu Khalid's deputies, and I expressed my anger about statements Abu Khalid made during the attack on the camps. I asked him to convey an angry message. I also had contact with our supporters in Ramallah and Birzeit in the West Bank. They were a good group of faculty and student activists. I asked them to think of disassociating with Fatah uprising. I was considering taking that move. Both conversations were conveyed to Abu Khalid. He became angry with me. A close friend and comrade, Saadi, who visited Damascus a few days later, came back and warned me against going to Damascus. But there was much anger bottled up in me. I did not really care. Making matters worse was our newspaper publication *al-Haqīqah,* Arabic for "The Truth." An activist student within our group published it, and we distributed it in the United States and mailed it to many activists in many other countries. It contained major articles and opinions. We all wrote articles, some harshly criticized the Syrian regime as well as Amal. Abu Khalid told me that during a meeting with Abdul Halim Khaddam, Syrian foreign minister, he later pulled out one of *al-Haqīqah* issues and presented it to Abu Khalid, and said, "You need to be aware of what your supporters in America are writing about us." I told Abu Khalid we will not embarrass him again like that.

Meanwhile, Fatah's old guard leadership knew of our group's major slowdown in activity. One day I received a strange phone call from the late Hatem Husseini. He was the PLO unofficial representative in the U.S. Hatem wanted to encourage me to rejoin Fatah supporters and officially disassociate myself and our group from the antileadership uprising. The leadership was engaged in a campaign to bring back all cadres who left and joined the uprising. I thanked him for his call but did not give any sign of willingness to take his advice. A couple of days later, I received a call from Fahmi, a local community leader, who informed me that Salah Tamari, a Fatah second-tier leader and Arafat loyalist, who was also married to former Queen

Dina of Jordan, King Hussein's ex-wife, was in the U.S. and wanted to come visit me for a meeting. Tension between the two Fatah opposing sides was very high at the time, however, I did not hold hatred and bitterness in my heart. I believed there was no problem in meeting with any of our former comrades.

Amjad, our former coordinator, was in San Diego by then. He was also invited to the meeting. Amjad fled Damascus during the war of camps without letting anyone know, including his close mentor and leader Abu Khalid, who suffered embarrassment over it. The meeting with Salah Tamari took place in my apartment. For over 2 hours of discussion, Tamari asked Amjad and me to rejoin the old guard leadership; in other words, declare our remorse and renew our loyalty. I was quick to tell Mr. Tamari that I was not interested in the old guard leadership any longer because we needed reform, political clarity, uprooting of corruption, and adherence to the founding principles and goals of the organization. Fatah was still on the same wrong path, so there was no reason for me to rejoin the old guard. Then I listened to Amjad respond and was surprised he had a much softer approach.

A couple of weeks later, Amjad was on his way to Tunis, the new headquarters of Fatah, and was back on track with the old leadership. All those who rejoined the old guard leadership never regained respect and remained on the periphery of Fatah and the PLO hierarchy. They made a living, but remained an outcast.

For the Palestinian American community, the split of Fatah caused a strategic blow. We went from being a very dynamic politically active community to a disintegrated one. It was never the same after our group and all its supporters quit. No other group was able to replace it. The vacuum we left was very large and was not filled for many years after.

Chapter 15

Hamas 1986, and the Intifada of the West Bank and Gaza

Fatah and all other PLO factions were much weaker after leaving Lebanon. Having no significant military arm marginalized the PLO political clout. The defeat of 1982 and Fatah antileadership uprising and split relatively delegitimized Palestinian representation. Fatah and the PLO leaders found themselves in the Tunisian capital Tunis, along with hundreds of cadres and military commanders who had no field to do their job. In the meantime, a new movement was on the rise filling the vacuum. That new movement had been there in most areas where Fatah existed, including the U.S. Yet, it had no part in the PLO structure or its activities. Its members worked quietly, recruited supporters, and preached its religious ideological approach to liberating Palestine. We only knew them as a Muslim Brotherhood group. They showed up sometimes in certain debates or lectures, only to contest by speaking out loud or shout slogans, which amounted to making a statement that all PLO factions, secular, socialist, and otherwise, were failures, and Islam was the only solution. We did not give them much attention. That movement was launched in Gaza, then the West Bank. Its name . . . "Hamas." In Arabic, the name makes up the initials of "Islamic Resistance Movement," which, when put together, made a word which meant "Enthusiasm." Sheikh Ahmed Yassin, a man paralyzed from the neck down due to an accident when he was younger, was its founder and spiritual leader. He was a leader with solid determination. While he was in Israeli captivity, the interrogators tortured his son almost to death right in front of his eyes. They wanted him to tell all he knew about the Hamas military wing, but he did not.

The Intifada of the West Bank and Gaza, 1987

Khalil al-Wazir, Arafat's Fatah second in command, was focused on the West Bank and Gaza Tanzim, as the last base of resistance. He spent a great deal of time and effort on working to strengthen and organize a large network, with a self-sustaining mechanism of leadership replacement so once the top leaders were arrested, their replacement was ready to take over. Both

Hamas and Fatah were racing to gain more support in the only two territories considered by the United Nations as "occupied territories." Their efforts showed results in the months that followed. The "Intifada" broke out. Pressures of Israeli occupation were mounting, and a massive popular uprising broke out on the streets. At first, it was thought of as demonstrations which might last a day or 2, and then it was clear that it was a longer campaign of popular defiance, with civil strikes and confrontations with the occupying force. It was a peaceful movement at first, followed by stone throwing at soldiers who retaliated with both rubber and live bullets, and who injured and killed ordinary men and women protestors.

For the first time in many years the Palestinian people of the West Bank and Gaza were out on the streets in massive numbers demanding freedom. Western and world media alike could no longer ignore such a movement of the people. It was no longer masked men, armed, who claimed to be freedom fighters while Israel and the Western countries called them terrorists. It was the people. Can anyone deny the people? Demonstrations and strikes spread to every city and town in the West Bank and Gaza day after day.

The Israeli government was not ready to deal with the new phenomena. It became known as "The Intifada," Arabic for "uprising of the people," as previously mentioned. At one time the Israeli government practiced the "Broken arm" punishment. If anyone was caught throwing stones at the IDF, IDF soldiers broke his arm with stones. When implemented, people all over the world watched on television as IDF soldiers, capturing a young student, sometimes just a young teenager, held his arm out while another soldier hammered it with rocks. Those images changed the Western world's perception of Israel. For the first time, Israel was shown as a true occupation force, which ruthlessly treated the population under its occupation. Even Israel's closest allies, governments of the United States and Western European countries, openly criticized Israel's policies for the first time. Finally, the world recognized Palestinians as a people, unified for also the first time after 40 years of denial.

Palestinian activists in all countries found themselves in a supportive position for a change. The struggle was initiated inside Palestine rather than elsewhere. Palestinians in the Diaspora and in Israel demonstrated in support of their people. It was sad for me and my comrades that we could not

321

mobilize the community as we had in the past. Instead, small personal initiatives were launched in different cities. It was nowhere near the events we used to organize and carry out before our split. I thought the Palestinian and Arab American community could have shown more significant support for the Intifada. The times when we were able to organize solidarity demonstrations in all U.S. major cities, on the same day, had disappeared.

At that time, we did not understand the significance of the Intifada. We were witnessing a strategic turning point of the Palestinian cause, and we did not know it. One thing we did know, and that was the Intifada would not lead to any true liberation.

I turned my focus to my professional career and tried to build a good personal future. I managed projects for a real estate development company and gave that most of my attention. I also thought about starting a family. I had a relationship with Ryana, a good woman. We met at the university, and we loved each other. I learned a lot from her. I never knew why we had such an attraction to each other. We had different personalities. Ryana was Mexican American. She came from a modest family, was an "A" student, pursued the American dream road map of success, and was very organized in almost everything she did. I, on the other hand, was considered a rebel in almost everything I did. I did not like to do anything if it was imposed on me, especially what I thought were little annoying things . . . like driving within the speed limit. Also, respecting time was a big challenge for me. I slept very late yet had to wake up early to attend my classes. I smoked cigarettes, she did not. I thought of my American experience as just a short period of my life. I did not see how Ryana could be part of my revolutionary Palestinian life, especially since I planned to be back in Beirut to rejoin my comrades. Eventually, Ryana and I separated, but could not stay away from each other. We tried again, but life had, by then, changed both of us. Ryana could not completely understand how that Palestinian revolutionary part of me pulled and pushed my life. She thought I did not know what I really wanted in life. So we just remained as good friends.

It was summer of 1988 when I was on vacation in Athens, Greece, that I met Randa. I knew her back when she was a teenage friend of my younger sister Salma, and despite the fact that we argued and seemed to resent each other during those years, deep down, I had a crush on her. It was 12 years since I last saw her in Beirut. She worked in Kuwait as an investment banker. Seeing her after all these years of being in the U.S. reinforced the thought that I needed to marry a woman from a very similar background. I was tired of the separation I had with my own culture, and wanted to feel at home in a marriage.

The vacation was memorable. We had a wonderful time with some friends on Skiathos, a beautiful Greek island. We were together a few days when I proposed to her, which was out of character for me. It used to take me a long time to decide on anything, but I did not want to lose her. I felt very strongly that our marriage was meant to be. We stayed in Greece through the first week of September, then I left for the U.S., and she went back to Kuwait. We met again a few days before our wedding in the beach city of Limassol, on the Mediterranean island of Cyprus. We were married on January 13, 1988, and our wedding was a very beautiful event. Both of our relatives flew in from different countries to be with us. A year and a half later, our daughter Layan was born.

I made a change of profession in 1991 from real estate development to mortgage. I started a company with a friend. I learned a lot about housing finance. Strangely, it was the profession which, a few years later, reconnected me with Palestine.

The Rise of Hamas

Hamas, during the Intifada, became more open to the Palestinian public, and it became more openly connected. It gained more supporters. The popular mood of the Arab people shifted in favor of Islamic movements as secular, nationalist, and socialist movements proved unsuccessful in making significant progress. Even the victory of the 1973 October war was not enough to boost its support. Sadat of Egypt was viewed as pro-American, and Hafez Assad of Syria was not viewed as a popular unifying Arab leader. The support base of all Pan-Arab movements was shrinking. The disintegration of the former Soviet Union produced even a stronger negative momentum to the weakening of those movements. After all, the USSR was their major supporter.

Contrary to Fatah which was relinquishing its armed struggle approach, Hamas made it a pillar strategy. They established Ezzedeen Al-Qassam brigades, named after the religious sheikh Qassam who led the Palestinian armed struggle against British mandate forces in the early 1930s. He was from Syria and was killed in a battle in the town of Ya'bad in the northeast portion of Palestine. He and his men fought to death and never surrendered when they were circled by British soldiers. He became a Palestinian icon.

Qassam brigades carried out many attacks against the IDF and later vowed to kill an Israeli every time a Palestinian was killed by the IDF. Eventually, violence and counterviolence escalated on both sides. Hamas proved to be a very serious threat to Israel, meanwhile, Fatah looked more and more moderate and became a counterpart in a never-ending negotiation process. Hamas's manifesto called for the liberation of all of Palestine with no compromise. Fatah moved to become an independence movement with land of the West Bank and Gaza considered as Palestine, and the other 78 percent of the land of Palestine recognized as Israel. Those main differences created a new polarization process of the Palestinian people.

The Intifada 1987 Palestinian Youth with Stones up against the IDF

Chapter 16

Madrid Conference and Oslo Accords

The Intifada and ongoing Hamas attacks pressured Israel's government at the time to look for a way to change the pattern of events. The United States had started a dialog with the PLO after it had to recognize Israel's right to exist and renounced terrorism in a declaration made by Yasser Arafat, who had to appear several times making this declaration in news conferences before the statement was found acceptable to the U.S. He read it, although his face showed a lot of irritation. In one interview he said in an answer to the question if that statement was enough: "What else do you want me to do—strip for you?" It must have been excruciating for Arafat to utter those words, since he himself was the main founder of Fatah, which considered military actions against Israel as "armed struggle," and those who were killed while engaged in it as martyrs. Most of the Palestinian people believed in that. Arafat's statement indirectly acknowledged the PLO used terrorism, however, he and the PLO leadership understood if they wanted to join any meaningful peace talks, the United States had to be a sponsor, and for the PLO to have any official contact with the U.S. government, the PLO had to meet those two conditions, dictated by U.S Congress and signed on by President Reagan.

Fatah and most of the PLO leadership did not publicly acknowledge the failure of armed struggle, albeit they acted it and seemed to have planned their political steps accordingly. The PLO did not believe it can revive armed struggle. All the leaders were under the complete security control of their host governments, which were moderate, pro-American, and did not want direct confrontation with Israel. On the other hand, Hamas was operating on the ground, in Palestine, and was not subject to any outside pressure.

In 1991, the United States and Soviet Union, with the support of Israel, Western countries, and their Arab allies, initiated the Madrid Peace Conference. After the opening meeting, delegations joined different negotiation tracks: the Syrian-Israeli track, Lebanese-Israeli track, and Jordanian-Palestinian-Israeli track. The Palestinian delegation was allowed to participate in a combined Jordanian-Palestinian delegation. Palestinian representatives had to be nonmembers of the PLO. That arrangement survived for some time before that track was split into two separate tracks: the Jordanian-Israeli track and a Palestinian-Israeli track. It was the first time such a conference took place where Israel and Arab countries and Palestinians met together. It was the beginning of the serious peace process. Even though the Syrians and Israelis did not reach an agreement, they came very close to it. The Jordanians and Israel came out with an agreement which became known as "Wadi Araba Treaty," referring to a border village area where the agreement was signed on October 26, 1994. Border, territory, and water disputes were settled along with mutual recognition and normalization of relations.

Oslo Peace Agreement between the PLO and Israel, August 1993

It became apparent during the Madrid conference that no moderate Palestinian delegation can truly represent the Palestinians without referring to the PLO, the only legitimate representative of the Palestinian people. The Israeli government realized it was negotiating with the PLO whether or not they acknowledged it. There was no way around the

PLO. Through secret channels, meetings were arranged and started in Norway, with the direct presence of PLO leaders and Israeli government representatives, Shimon Peres and Yasser Arafat, who supervised those talks. At some point they both were on the same phone conference, as Peres mentioned in the documentary *The 50 Years War: Israel and the Arabs*. Though they did not speak directly to each other, they heard each other's voices on speaker presenting certain points.

The main front Palestinian negotiator was Ahmed Qurei, commonly known as "Abu Alaa," not a founding member of the top-level leadership of Fatah, but for sure, was in the close circle of Arafat. He was also known as a moneyman. He managed investments for Fatah in different countries. He was also the head of "Samed," an establishment which made clothing and Palestinian artifacts. It was supposed to employ martyrs' families. Behind Abu Alaa was Mahmoud Abbas, (Abu Mazin), who later succeeded Arafat in leadership. He was very involved in negotiations which went on until the parties reached the "Declaration of Principles." It was an agreement which allowed the creation of a self-rule government in the West Bank and Gaza, named the "Palestinian Authority" (PA). The negotiating parties agreed to a staged implementation. West Bank and Gaza territories were classified as Zones A, B, and C, for purposes of definition of security and administrative roles of the Palestinian Authority and Israeli military rule . . . way short of any sovereignty for the Palestinians. Based on the agreement, an interim phase was supposed to be implemented until a final settlement was reached.

News of the breakthrough agreement came. Except for those who knew what was going on, it caught Palestinians everywhere by surprise. Most concerned people wanted to know the details of the agreement. Many rumors were circulating of secret addendums which contained major obligations and concessions.

It was obvious to me and my comrades that Oslo was a sellout of Palestine. We felt somewhat ashamed that it was happening during our lifetime. The Palestinian cause was, for the first time, being sold out in parts . . . by Palestinians, no less. It was devastating.

I suddenly recalled an argument I had a year before with Nimr, a second-tier Fatah leader, a well-known advisor and spokesperson who ran Fatah's radio during the heated battles of the late sixties and seventies. I met him in Jordan coincidentally while visiting a relative. He and a group of Fatah Revolutionary Council members were present. They were speaking of Fatah's victories, and seemed to be very proud of their party's achievements. I thought to myself, *What world do they live in?* I tried to stay out of it, but I just could not. I found myself talking and said that I believed a victory or defeat is measured by set goals and objectives, and I asked them all to tell me which of the goals and objectives stated in Fatah and the PLO charters have been achieved? I believed none. That was the time Nimr intervened and addressed my points, of course, first by trying to discredit them by saying opposing PLO factions and Hamas have the same position. I made it clear to them that I was, at that point, totally independent and didn't have any affiliation with them. Nimr proceeded by explaining that the Israelis have ceded in many ways, and that was the first time I heard of the land classifications A, B, and C. He did not elaborate what those classifications meant at the time. I knew a year or so later when the Oslo Accords were published.

All factions, groups, and individuals who did not give up on the struggle for Palestine were in their weakest state: discouraged, disorganized, financially broke, and had no friendly Arab country to host and encourage their presence and activities. The end of the cold war and the breakup of the former Soviet Union was a major contributor to their marginalization. The Syrian regime opposed the Oslo Accords, but were not very confrontational about it.

Hafez Assad was known as a master politician. Just 2 years earlier, his regime participated in the multinational force led by the United States in the war to liberate Kuwait from Saddam Hussein's Iraqi occupying forces. He knew political tides had changed. He needed to position himself and his regime in a place of no isolation; he needed the Arab Gulf regimes to be on his side more than ever. The Syrian regime maintained a solid stand in peace negotiations and did not compromise on its sovereignty. It strengthened its alliance with Iran, Lebanon's Hezbollah, and Palestinian factions opposed to the Oslo Accords like Hamas.

One of the major consequences of the Oslo Accords was that it mostly confined the Palestinian cause to the West Bank and Gaza. They were referred to as Palestinian territories, later as the one and only Palestine. They agreed to cede 78 percent of the land of historical Palestine to the state of Israel in exchange for a geographically separated territory as a potential state. It also marginalized the right of Palestinians in the Diaspora, including refugees of the 1948 and 1967 war, and they became a refugee problem. Israel wanted them to permanently reside anywhere on earth—except their original cities, towns, and villages. They wanted the Palestinians to be granted citizenship in their host countries, and perhaps receive some compensation for the loss of their homes and homeland, Palestine. There was only a hope that the newly defined Palestine (West Bank and Gaza) would someday become a state, and some of the Palestinian refugees just might—or not—get the right at some time to reside in it and consider it a homeland. But again, that would be part of the final peace settlement yet to arrive.

Palestinians in the Diaspora knew they were way on the bottom of the list of priorities. As for Palestinians inside Israel, commonly known as Arab Israelis, the PLO and the New Palestinian Authority officially have almost nothing to do with them, as if they are not Palestinians. They should remain a minority, struggling for their rights in their homeland, albeit, they must understand they live in a Jewish state, and therefore, accept they are, in many ways, second-class citizens, and are not treated by the same standards as a Jewish citizen of a Jewish state. The Oslo Accords stripped the PLO of its representative power of all Palestinians, and then transformed it into a paralyzed, shallow body—used, if needed, and ignored most of the time. For the first time, our people were divided. The oneness and unity of the Palestinians were shattered. The leadership accepted to redefine Palestine, and redefine who is a Palestinian. The virtual lines dividing our people became acceptable by the PLO leadership.

Fatah leadership was consistent with its past. They found ambiguity in the Oslo Accords verbiage, enough for them to interpret it in a way which claimed they did not give away Palestinian embraced rights. More so, Fatah and the PLO leadership never called for a referendum of the Palestinian people to approve or disapprove the Accords' fundamental impact on our lives and our future generations. Instead, only the PLO national parliament, whose mandate had long since expired, met and approved the Oslo Accords for the people. The fact is the PLO leadership structure was not much different from a totalitarian regime. They controlled the means of maintaining power, with no free elections to transfer leadership to new leaders.

Oslo Accords Era Begins, Arafat in Gaza

The historic agreement found its way to implementation in a relatively short time. Offices for the Palestinian Preventative Security Force were set up preceding official entry of PLO leadership and personnel, underscoring that security was the cornerstone of the Accords. Colonels Jibril Rajoub and Mohammed Dahlan were appointed security chiefs of the West Bank and Gaza, respectively. Neither were well-known to Palestinian activists abroad, however, they were recognized inside the Palestinian territories. They had both been political prisoners and local leaders of Fatah activists inside and outside of prison. Their new appointment included responsibility for preventing Palestinian attacks against Israel.

Chairman Arafat came into Gaza on July 1, 1994. He was well received by the people, and it was a historic and celebrated day. In his speeches, he addressed concerns that even though the Accords gave the PLO control of Gaza and Jericho, more territories will be under Palestinian government. Palestinians were desperate for victory. The scene itself was enough to create an overwhelming feeling of liberation and triumph. People wanted to believe peace was happening.

Soon, other Palestinian cities were handed to the newly created Palestinian Authority. All major cities and towns of the West Bank and Gaza were classified as Territory "A." In other words, the PA was in control where populations existed, noncontiguous enclaves. When traveling from one city or town to another, one had to go through areas "B" and "C," which meant Israeli security checkpoints. Getting into Israel, Jordan, and Egypt required a special Israeli permit, even for the chairman of the PA himself. VIP permits were issued by Israel for PLO officials, and those were rated by higher ranks. The rating defined certain privileges like traveling with a car or without one, etc.

It was not too long before PA security forces cracked down on Hamas and other factions, and anyone who believed in, and planned for, armed struggle against Israel. The term "Land for Peace," which Israeli leaders used over and again, meant to concede land for peace. It was mocked by some Israeli politicians who demanded it be changed to "Land for Security." Many Hamas and other activists were jailed and tortured by PA security forces, which created grudges that lasted for a long time. On the other hand, Palestinians liked and supported the idea of being ruled by their fellow Palestinians.

Symbols of Sovereignty

Israeli negotiators never promised the Palestinians a state. They just considered the Accords as an interim agreement which should lead to a final settlement. From the start, Israel was not agreeable to even the smallest symbols of sovereignty. The PA, for example, has no "president," but rather, a "chairman." Luckily, both words in Arabic mean "president," which made it acceptable to Arafat to be addressed as chairman, and in Arabic, president. Arafat built around him all aspects of presidency. He had reception ceremonies, presidential guard units, and many other practices which implied the PA was transforming into a government of a potentially sovereign Palestinian state. Israel did not mind that . . . within limits . . . and as long as nothing really changed, that remained a facade.

Economic boom and opportunities improved. People's standard of living improved. Projects were very significant, both in the public and private sectors of the economy, with support of donor countries. Palestinian entrepreneurs increased, especially those known regionally and internationally. Owners of multibillion-dollar companies multiplied, and they got the lion's share of the newly emerging economy. Projects of telecommunication, electricity, banking, industry, hotels, car dealerships, etc., were mostly owned by them. In addition, PA monopolies were created for essential products like cement, steel, petroleum, and cigarettes.

Arafat , Clinton and Rabin, Oslo Accord signing Ceremony 1993

Chapter 17

Heading to Palestine, a Different Kind of Return

The thought of visiting Palestine during my lifetime was unimaginable before then. I was addicted to following the news and was emotionally moved when I watched the opening of an international airport in Gaza. Somehow, I thought the interim peace agreement was accumulating peace one piece at a time between two longtime enemies. One day, I received an unexpected phone call from a friend, an entrepreneur, who had set up a business in Palestine. He told me that a major project to establish a mortgage company in Palestine was being planned, and that he had recommended that I manage it. My immediate reaction was not positive. I told him that I did not believe I could work for the Palestinian Authority since it was mostly made up of people from Fatah who stuck by the old guard leadership while I supported the mutiny. I also knew how they were structured and how they functioned. I did not think I could work professionally and accomplish much. He stressed that I should send him my résumé, even if I did not intend to go, just because he had promised them that I would and he was counting on our close relationship. I did not even have a résumé. But I was self-employed, and I had owned my business for a few years. However, not to embarrass my friend, I put together a résumé and faxed it to him. The next thing I knew, people from the World Bank contacted me and asked to meet me. A senior advisor for the World Bank who was involved in the project was from San Diego. He called me. He had just come back from Palestine. We met, he liked me, and endorsed me. I was invited to go to Palestine and meet the stakeholders of the project.

In Tel Aviv

It was December 1998, during the holiday season. I was on a plane which landed in Tel Aviv close to midnight. What a feeling! I was confused about whether this was real or was I dreaming. Here I was—with all my background and hard-core commitment to the Palestine cause—in Tel Aviv, talking to Israelis at the customs checkpoint—as an American citizen. Thoughts rushed in my head about what would I say if they had my name in their database. It would not have been strange as some countries keep data going back more than 20 years at airports, and they sometimes give people a hard time. Strangely, the questions were normal and I was let through.

I did not see the driver who was supposed to meet me, so I made a phone call and was assured he was on the way from Jerusalem to pick me up and take me to a hotel in Ramallah; I went to the airport terminal café, and while having coffee I noticed I was sitting next to four Israeli soldiers, part of airport security. They were chatting and laughing. How ironic. I never thought I would be this close to any Israeli soldier except on a battlefield. Life had obviously changed.

The driver finally showed up. The drive to Ramallah was over an hour. I was looking out the car window from the time I sat in the passenger seat until we arrived at the hotel. I could not get enough of the view. We passed by a few small towns and villages and soon arrived at the Grand Park Hotel in Ramallah. Even though it was around 2:30 A.M., I could not sleep. I was very anxious for the daylight to break.

In the early-morning hours I was looking out the window when the sun began to rise. Later, Deputy Minister Abdelmajeed came to the hotel and picked me up. We were on our way to meet the regional manager of Arab Bank, who was also the vice chairman of the board of directors. The meeting went well. Mr. Shaker Basshur was a very influential man, carrying the weight of responsibility of the largest and probably oldest bank in the country and the Arab region. He was pleased with me and granted his approval for the board to hire me as the founding chief executive officer of the mortgage company to be created.

That afternoon, I had another important meeting with Angela Iutsky. She was the country representative of the International Finance Corporation, a subsidiary of the World Bank, which invests in public and private sector partnership projects in many developing countries. The meeting was in Jerusalem, so I took a taxi there. Upon seeing the Dome of the Rock I had an overwhelming magical feeling come over me as the car went down the hill, entering one of holiest cities on earth.

My meeting with Ms. Iutsky was at the American Colony Hotel. Unlike its name, the hotel building is

Arabic and Islamic in architecture. It was popular among journalists and expatriates who wanted to get a feel of the Palestinian life in East Jerusalem. Our meeting lasted 7 hours. It felt like I met my match, someone, who, like me, once he or she likes a project, can discuss it endlessly. We created a virtual scenario of how the company would be put together and how it would function. There was no mortgage market in the Palestinian territories and no existing model in nearby Jordan or Egypt at the time. Israel had a different model than what was envisaged by the World Bank. Samara then asked me when I was going to start. I told her I was not sure yet, that I would need to think about it. She then laid a serious guilt trip on me. She told me that she was half English, half Swiss, and there she was, committed to help the Palestinians through development projects, so how is it that I, a Palestinian, was hesitant to begin this much-needed mortgage project? That question hit me hard. I promised Samara that I was only going to think of how to make it happen.

In the evening I was back at the hotel, then I had another meeting with Abdelmajeed. This time he was more eager to get me to commit. He even made a phone call to Chairman Arafat's office and wanted to take me to meet him. The idea was for me to commit in front of the chairman, something which would have erased any hesitation I might have had. I had caught the flu while in Ramallah, and I used that as an excuse that I just did not want to pass my flu on to the chairman, since hugs and cheek kisses are a Palestinian custom when greeting someone you like and respect. Mr. Abdelmajeed was not totally convinced, but did not insist.

Acre, at Last

The next day I was all set and ready to go. I was very excited to finally see Acre, our hometown. Friends insisted they drive me there. We arrived a few hours later. It was already dark, but we still drove through the narrow streets of the ancient city. My friend asked me if I wanted to go someplace in particular. I thought of "Abu Khristo," the name of a restaurant my father told me about. That's where he and his friends used to hang out in their earlier years. We stopped the car, and I asked a man on the street if that restaurant was still there, and he said, "Yes, for sure," and he explained how to get there. Khristo is a Greek name. The owner was a Greek immigrant to Palestine, and that was his son's name, and therefore, it was called "Abu Khristo,"

346

"the father of Khristo." My two friends and I went into the restaurant and sat at a table. I closely observed the place and looked into every corner, imagining that my father, my grandfather, my uncle Rafik were sitting in that place, drinking, talking, joking, and laughing, celebrating good things in life in that place. We had dinner and a couple of drinks, then they dropped me off at a hotel right outside the city wall to the south.

In the morning I walked out of my room, on the sixth floor. The elevator hall had a huge window, and I was amazed looking out at the old city of Acre standing there just as I imagined it—its houses, its mosques, churches, castle, prison, and so many historical places, all circled by a great wall touching the Mediterranean Sea. It was a view I will remember for the rest of my life. Shortly after, I took a taxi and asked the driver to drop me off anywhere in the old city. The driver said, "How about al-Jazzar Mosque?" I said, "Yes, that would be good."

In front of the entrance to the great mosque, I got out of the taxi with my video camera and started filming. I walked right behind two Western tourists into the courtyard of the mosque, where I saw an old man. I greeted him, he greeted me back, and I said, "My family is originally from Acre." I was hoping he would know about my family and point me to the neighborhood they used to live in. That would have pleased me; after all, it had been 50 years since they left. The old man asked me, "What's your family's name?" "Ammouri," I said. He asked, "Where do they live?" I said, "Beirut." "So are you Hasan's son or someone else?" I was stunned! I said, "Yes, I am Hasan's son." Standing close to him was another old man. He tapped him on the shoulder and told him, "Accompany him. Show him where his father's shop used to be and bring him back here." Then he told me, "When you come back I will introduce you to the mosque's director. He will tell you all about what happened in Acre since your family left."

We walked outside and around the area. It was a 5-minute walk between street venders and shoppers. In front of small shops, Arabic music filled the air, as well as smoke from burned mesquite charcoal mixed with grilled lamb meat. Moving cars almost rubbed against my arm.

"That was sahat Abboud," (Abboud square) the old man pointed at a shop which looked like a furniture shop. He said, "That used to be your father's shop." From there we walked again to Souq al-Abyad, the

White Market. It was a historical building with an arched white ceiling. We walked into it, and he pointed to a closed shop and said, "That was your uncle's shop."

From there we walked back to the mosque where I met the director, who welcomed me and told me about the changes that happened to Acre, mostly demographic, and how it was still over 90 percent Palestinians, however a great majority were people who moved in from the nearby villages, since Acre was empty of more than three-quarters of its original inhabitants of pre-1948 days. That day was a Friday, and it was Christmas Day as well. Traditional Friday prayers were going on in the mosque hall. The director said, "There will be a gathering here in my office after the prayer, then we go all together and wish our Christian brothers a Merry Christmas. Shortly, I will introduce you to a relative of yours."

I remembered my family used to talk of how Christians and Muslims in Acre celebrated each other's holidays and lived together in great harmony. I told the director, "I don't think we still have relatives here." He said, "Just hang around and we'll see about that."

After the prayer, around 20 men came into the director's office. He called out, "Mohammad, come here." The man came over to us. The director looked at me and the man, in turn, and said to me, "This is Mohammad al-Halawani." I did not know how that made the man a relative of mine until the director continued, "His grandmother's name is Shafeeqa Ammouri. She was your grandfather's sister." I was astonished.

Mohammad and I shook hands. I told him who I was, and I was a little embarrassed that he knew my father, my uncles, and a lot more than I knew about him. Mohammad and I spent the afternoon together. We walked the streets and alleys. He showed me my parents' old home, a small, two-story building. It was deserted. The top floor ceiling had caved in due to many years of no maintenance. He also showed me my uncle Rafik's home, where he lived with his family, and where he also died. We passed by my grandfather's home, and finally, we went into his home which was his grandmother's home before. I met his wife and kids. They made me tea. I asked him about my cousins and if he knew their whereabouts after my uncle had passed away. He did not know, but said their old neighbor knows, a Christian lady. Her name was Um Ilyas. She had moved to the new part of the city, however, an owner of a nearby restaurant would know how to reach her. He was a friend of the family.

We went to that restaurant. The man was nice. He called Um Ilyas and told her that I was in town and looking for my cousins. He then passed the phone receiver to me. I talked to the lady. She asked me to go to her home and gave me directions. I thanked the restaurant owner, took a taxi, and headed to Um Ilyas's home. She was very hospitable, offered me some coffee, and while I was sipping it, she dialed a telephone number and said, "Here, talk to your cousin." Suha was the oldest daughter of my uncle. She lived in San Jose, California, with her husband and son. There I was in Acre, talking to my cousin who lived so close to me in California, and neither of us knew it! She sounded happy, and she also encouraged me to talk to her sister Nada, who lived, along with her other sisters and brothers, in a Jerusalem neighborhood. Right after my conversation with Suha, Um Ilyas called Nada. We spoke, but it was hard to communicate. Nada seemed to have forgotten a lot of her childhood Arabic. We managed to exchange phone numbers. I told her I was heading back to the U.S. and would most likely be back to take the job and be stationed in Ramallah, and that I was really hoping to meet her soon afterward. I thanked Um Ilyas and left. The next day, I was on my way back to San Diego.

To Go or Not to Go

I thought long and hard about my anticipated move for the job, a move I was sure would add stress to my marriage. My son Walid was only 10 months old. My wife and I named him after my late brother. My daughter Layan was almost 10 years old. After discussions with my wife and some relatives, I decided to take the job and go to Palestine. More important, I felt it was my calling, despite all my personal concerns as well as worries of how I was going to cope with the political and social environment.

It was a very cold and rainy morning. I woke up and was ready to go. My heart sank as my travel became real. I hugged and kissed Layan and Randa, then I went into Walid's room. He was sleeping. I kissed him and said, "I love you, son. I'm sorry I have to go, but I will be back." I took a flight to Ottawa, Canada, where I attended a few days' orientation with the Canada Mortgage and Housing Corporation, the technical advisor of the project, with a generous donation from the Canadian government. Most of the top executive directors of CMHC were ready, willing, and able to help me and my new management team. Palestine Mortgage and Housing Corporation was envisioned to be a smaller model of the Canadian government-owned CMHC. Deputy Minister Abdelmajeed met me in Ottawa. I felt the Canadians wanted the project to succeed as one of their many efforts to help the Palestinian people build their homeland and eventually, a state. We had many technical meetings as well as many formal receptions. Two senior executives of CMHC were designated as full-time advisors in the field. They had moved to Ramallah before I had and were just waiting for the new CEO and the management team to arrive and start implementing the well prepared business plan and create the new housing finance company. From Ottawa I took a flight to Tel Aviv. This time it was more familiar, and from there, to Ramallah, and that was the first day of a 4-year journey in the old homeland.

Time for Hard Work

I was focused on trying to make a difference, add value to people's life in Palestine, build something unique, something my people can look at as a good model of how a modern, successful economic institution was built. Within a short time, the company proved to have been managed professionally, recruited with no favoritism, and conducted business with no corruption. We did all we could to help people by making it easier for Palestinians who had been waiting for years to be able to buy a home or build one. The idea and the practice were both premature for implementation in Palestinian territories governed by the PA, however, I knew myself, once I get attached to a cause, I give it my best efforts, and the Palestine Mortgage and Housing Corporation was my new cause and my baby. I was much more attached to it than the shareholders themselves. After all, they were big entities—the World Bank, the Palestinian Authority, and a group of the largest regional banks and large companies. The World Bank was represented by Angela lutsky, who was the main driver, and Abdel Majeed, deputy minister of housing who worked hard with the PA to make it happen. I felt most of the other shareholders were, for good or bad, dragged into it. Not many believed it would succeed, especially since the project was talked about for a long time before, and no launching had ever taken place. People thought it was dead in the water.

The economy was developing, but it lacked certain fundamentals to allow for such a project to succeed, yet, we hoped it would catch up with the company. I was full of energy, motivation, drive, and inspiration to make it materialize. People felt it and witnessed my determination and implementation steps taken in a short time. Naturally, some people did not want it to succeed, simply because they were not part of it, had no gain from it, and no clout over it. Community leaders, builders, entrepreneurs, unions, professors, teachers, government employees, and political activists were very excited to see a housing finance source established to help thousands, as there were many unfinished dwellings, and many could not even start building due to a lack of residential affordable lending. Scarce loans existed for only a short term and high rates.

I had many meetings and was invited to several gatherings of those groups, where I explained the PMHC lending model, how people could utilize and generate opportunities of growth and employment through demand for goods and services of the local economy. I worked long into the night in my Ramallah office; my creativity was flowing like never before, which helped me find solutions to many complicated projects, which were not part of the American or Canadian mortgage lending system, including the cooperatives system which had specific bylaws and does not subdivide members' properties, and kept the ownership title in the name of the cooperative, which made it impossible to mortgage any specific member's property to secure a long-term loan.

I was successful in creating several mortgage lending programs which were customized to the local housing environment. My high-profile position as a CEO led me to meet most of the leaders of the PA and the Palestinian society as a whole, and many of the well-known people came to visit me asking for my help to secure financing either for their own homes or those of their colleagues and supporters of the same party, organization, or society. Sometimes the pressure was too much to handle. Many leaders did not like how the mortgage programs not only tied up their property but also restricted their monthly salaries in a way that the mortgage payment was deducted from it first, then the rest of the salary was released to the borrower. I had to include such a condition for it was tough to chase down a leader or a minister should he not make his payment. I could not imagine the mortgage company foreclosing on him, or even make it public knowledge that such an important leader was not making his payments. Letting anyone get away without payment could have caused major loss of credibility to the new and important PMHC, which was supposed to be an advanced development financial model.

Preparations to launch activities went on for months. Doubts started to be cast again as to whether the PMHC would ever start giving out mortgage loans. First there was a hold on an incentive needed from the Palestine Monetary Authority (PMA), an equivalent to a central bank in a sovereign country. However, the Palestinian Authority did not issue a currency. The PMA's role was mostly regulating banks, including issuing bank and bank branch licenses. The governor at the time of the PMA refused to grant the incentive. Many meetings took place without a resolution until the World Bank and IFC urged Chairman Arafat to interfere. He did. A meeting was held in Gaza at the office of Dr. Nabil Shaath, minister of planning at the time. The meeting included Dr. Salam Fayyad, who was the country's representative of the International Monetary Fund, Muayyad Mushid, a controversial personality, economic advisor to Arafat, as well as the CEO of the PCSC, which owned most of the investment holdings of the PA, Amin Haddad, PMA governor, Abdel Majeed, deputy housing minister, Angela lutsky, IFC country representative and the World Bank country representative.

The meeting reached a solution that opened the door for the shareholders to fund their capital contribution and put the new company in motion. I proceeded to make agreements with all the banks in West Bank and Gaza, an agonizing process which took much longer than I anticipated. It was a few months of back-and-forth, except for one bank where the CEO was strong enough and encouraging of the new housing finance system. Otherwise, even some banks who were major shareholders took longer due to legal worries and a superconservative approach to risk management. The idea seemed premature to those professionals who were in the heart of the lending sector. Even after concluding all the agreements which offered the banks little to no risk, it was still a struggle to get them to process and approve mortgage borrowers' applications, even though most of the borrowers had more than required equity in their homes.

I grew frustrated and thought of a way to get around the sluggish process and create a more effective processing and funding mechanism. I approached the public directly, placed ads in the major newspapers, and asked the potential borrowers to come directly to the PMHC offices, where I had prepared the specialized staff to meet them, help complete their applications and required documentation, and when they qualified, we issued a preapproval and sent them, with completed package, to the bank, which should have made their job much easier. Still, some banks tangled the applications in their bureaucracy and took weeks before they would grant their final commitment to the borrower. I hoped with time the process would become a regular routine, especially when everyone feels secure about the quality of the system we put in place. I made sure the Palestinian mortgage borrowers' default would be for extremely difficult circumstances where a borrower, for example, would be out of job for at least 6 months. Otherwise, most other causes of default borrowers were mitigated. The company started gaining a lot of popularity, especially through the local media and the many seminars we continued to organize which explained the new housing finance system.

Chapter 18

Oslo Accords Disappointment and Second Intifada

It was a period of overall economic growth and business activities boom which created many jobs, but most were not long term. The economy was not being built to create a strong middle class. And, most important, during all my working time in Palestine, I never heard of any economic plan to build an economy which meets the needs of the Palestinians. Although there were many projects being accomplished, there was no comprehensive plan.

In addition, Israel controlled all import entries and export exits, and collected the customs fees. They transferred the funds to the PA when they were satisfied with the PA, and withheld funds when they wanted to punish the PA. More than half the annual expense budget of the PA was contributed by Western donor countries, and most of the PA government institutions were being supervised and monitored by the U.S. and European countries.

Influence and control were called "institution building." Facts on the ground did not support the claim of building a future sustainable state for the people of Palestine.

Public sector employees, most of whom spent a good portion of their lives serving the cause of Palestine, became totally dependent on their salaries and that affected what they stood for in the new era. Most of those I met and talked to told me they were looking to settle down. They felt they had finally arrived at the place of their journey struggle, and they wanted to finally harvest the field they planted and took care of for the best part of their lives. That was their wishful thinking. They just completely ignored the facts staring them in the face, facts they came in touch with on a daily basis. The IDF was in full control. For example, when they traveled between one Palestinian city or town and another, if they wanted to visit nearby Jordan, or if they wanted to import a product from another country, it would most likely be stuck at the Israeli port in a prolonged customs process—not because anything was wrong with it, but most likely due to the fact that Israeli products sold to the Palestinians constituted by far the greatest in volume as compared to products made elsewhere. It was a way of supporting the Israeli economy and minimizing competition with products imported from other countries, which effectively discouraged importing from abroad and limited choices for Palestinians to buy. I was once told by an international economic expert that the Paris agreement was an official rape of the Palestinian economy. The Palestinians lived in a big prison: entry, exit, and duration of stay in or out was controlled by Israeli authorities at will.

The Second Intifada (Al-Aqsa Intifada)

In July of 2000, President Clinton had invited Yasser Arafat and Ehud Barak, then prime minister of Israel, to Camp David in hopes of reaching a final solution to the Palestinian-Israeli conflict. Arafat found himself isolated and surrounded by the United States and all its allies and was pressured to give up on major issues like Jerusalem and the right of return of Palestinian refugees, something he knew would completely tarnish his national image in the eyes of his people and end his legacy. However, even more important, Arafat himself did not believe for a split second on giving up the holy city of Jerusalem. Arafat was a devout Muslim. He did not comply with the terms and was blamed by Clinton as the spoiler of a potential deal. Arafat felt he was bullied and completely disrespected. It was obvious by his demeanor and words at the time. He had, for a long time, been diplomatic and was no longer interested in holding back. When asked by a reporter about what he thought of Barak and his offers, he responded, "Let him go to hell." When he came back to the West Bank, he was received with tremendous love and support of his people. Even those longtime opponents and critics, including myself, found ourselves having respect for Arafat, who stood up and refused to go down as a leader who sold out Jerusalem and the historic rights of his people.

On September 28, 2000, Ariel Sharon was not in government, but he was a main leader of the opposition party, the Likud. He decided to make a visit to Al-Aqsa Mosque compound at a time of intense Palestinian frustration and disappointment in the peace process. Sharon was good at seizing the moment to create big events. He proved it when he led the 1982 all-out invasion of Lebanon. His visit was an act of insult and intimidation of the Palestinians' most hated Israeli leader, for he was considered a ruthless warmongering general, associated with massacres. Confrontation broke out between the Muslim worshipers and demonstrators who came to protest Sharon's unwelcomed visit to the holy site. Then, demonstration protests broke out throughout all the West Bank and Gaza cities, towns, and villages. The IDF deployed its troops and military vehicles. The scene quickly became similar to that of the 1987 First Intifada.

My office was located in Albeireh, a town attached to Ramallah. I could see the clashes between Palestinian youngsters and the IDF at the Beit Eil Checkpoint, which guarded an Israeli base hosting the occupation civil administration department, a military court, and a temporary jail for Palestinian activists. The first few days of clashes, Palestinians threw stones toward the well equipped IDF. The IDF responded by firing tear gas grenades and sometimes hosed down the youngsters with water. Then the IDF decided to raise the stakes. They focused on one particular youngster who seemed more active than the others and shot him with a sniper's live bullet. The youngster fell, and his friends came running. They picked him up and put him in an ambulance which had just arrived. The ambulance whisked him off to a hospital. We didn't know if they killed him or not. That act was repeated almost daily. It was heartbreaking to watch. Those Palestinian kids who had no fear and were being slaughtered.

For a few days and at many hot spots of clashes between the IDF and the demonstrators, the death toll of shot youngsters rose. It was obvious the IDF was intent on scaring the Palestinian activists and forcing them to quit. The strategy did not work. Palestinians who had access to guns brought them to the clash points. When a Palestinian was shot, an armed Palestinian shot back at the IDF, and suddenly, what was supposed to be unarmed protests became armed ones, which gave the IDF an even better excuse to shoot and kill.

In the dark of the night, young Palestinians with light arms tried to put up a fight against one of the most professional armies in the world, the IDF. While driving to my apartment I found myself among a dozen youngsters who liked the location of the building I lived in, Masyoon Hill, because it overlooked a large part of Ramallah and Jerusalem. They fired a few shots from the hill in the direction of the IDF armored vehicles located far in the distance. I was sure they never hurt anyone since their light arms bullets would not even reach that far, however, the IDF responded with midrange machine guns. Three bullets blew through my apartment while I was sleeping. I lived on the top-floor apartment. It was surrounded with glass windows. It was totally exposed, and there was nothing to protect me from flying bullets. I could hardly sleep during the unfair exchange that went on until the early-morning hours almost every single night. I was lucky the IDF did not shoot at me while I was driving home around the edge of the hill. It was not too long before the IDF fired tank rockets at the hill. I decided to move into another apartment right in the heart of downtown Ramallah. I thought it was safer . . . and it was . . . but not for long. Clashes only got worse by the day.

Life in Ramallah, Jerusalem, as well as all other parts of the West Bank and Gaza had changed. It went from bustling and crowded to too quiet. Much of the crowd disappeared. People who used to frequent Ramallah from all over the West Bank did not come anymore. Palestinian Israelis used to visit, spend weekends, shop, and enjoy the entertainment, but they no longer showed up. Many ongoing projects were halted. Planned future projects froze. It seem that only funerals, demonstrations, and tension took over.

Tanzim party, which consisted of mostly armed members of Fatah, as well as civilian dressed security services known as the Preventive Security Forces which provides intelligence services, became more apparent on the streets and in cafés, while uniformed police and traffic officers all but disappeared. Israeli reconnaissance drones circled the sky. Many times an Apache helicopter or two flew for a few hours over Ramallah, then fired a rocket which most people, including myself, heard and knew that it was aimed at some Palestinian activist, marked for assassination. Everyone wondered whose life just ended by that rocket explosion that day. The news came out just a few minutes later.

Getting out of Ramallah into Jerusalem became a half-day waiting task at the Qalandya Israeli Checkpoint, where the stop and pass motion was conducted by one IDF soldier, and, it appeared, that motion depended on the soldier's mood. At times, an hour would crawl by before he or she would allow a single car to cross. The number of cars crossing each day was decided by the higher-ups in the Israeli defense ministry. They studied patterns and made their decisions. People who lived in the towns and villages outside Ramallah could not get to their jobs in the morning, or get home at the end of the day without being several hours late because of this delay. Many times they were just turned back and not allowed to enter.

One time at the Qalandya crossing, I was the next person to pass through from Ramallah headed to Jerusalem, and I was kept waiting 5 hours at night while the IDF soldier just stared at me. I could not even go to a restroom. I felt my bladder was about to explode, and I could not do anything about it. I was then living at a hotel in Jerusalem, and I had no choice but to wait. But that was not much to complain about when I thought of the pregnant women in labor who, more than once, gave birth at the checkpoints while waiting to cross and go to a hospital, or the patients in severe pain who waited to cross on their way to see their doctor on the other side, or university students who could not get to their classes when their university was located right adjacent to the city or town they lived in, like Birzeit University. IDF checkpoint soldiers had the authority and exercised it in an unpredictable manner.

The Second Intifada became a new reality, and that did not look like it was going to change anytime soon after. The Palestinians grew more frustrated and disappointed in the peace process. The Oslo Accords and their outcome embodied in the Palestinian Authority looked like an end, rather than a means to self-determination and statehood. On the Israeli side, voices of mistrust came out strong with the a message to the Israeli people that "we let the Palestinians rule themselves and brought the PLO in the country and allowed them to have guns— only to have them turn their guns on us—again." Palestinian suicide attacks against civilian targets scared Israelis regarding all Palestinians and did not help their image worldwide. Again, frustration and desperate acts ruled. Those young suicide bombers were totally convinced they were serving their people and were obviously willing to sacrifice their lives for their cause, however, their leadership did not only send them to military targets and that was a repeat of the early seventies' strategy which cost the Palestinian cause a great deal of support in the world. It is extremely difficult to find Palestinian public criticism of suicide bombings, not because of support for the action itself, but rather for the knowledge that the bombers who were killed as well were young Palestinians who believed they were sacrificing themselves for the sake of God and their people. Hamas and Jihad movements both, later, without declaration, seemed to have changed strategy and focused on fighting the IDF in soldier-to-soldier confrontations and stopped suicide bombings in civilian areas.

Ariel Sharon Is Back

Confrontations between Palestinians and the IDF seemed to have no end in sight. In addition to shooting incidents and suicide bombings, both the majority of Israeli and Palestinian public gave up on the peace process. Arafat himself seemed totally disappointed with the process and gave his blessings to individuals and groups who believed in rearming. He appeared to send an unspoken message to his people which amounted to a punch line, that he had failed in achieving a dignified Palestinian state or any symbolic form of the right of return. Activists watched and acted on that. They even founded new organized military groups which did not exist before the Second Intifada, like al-Aqsa Martyrs' Brigades.

An Israeli special election was held in February 2001. Likud, Ariel Sharon's party, won the majority, which led to Sharon becoming the prime minister. He formed his government on March 7, 2001, and did not wait long. He knew exactly what he wanted to do. The Israeli air force carried out strikes on all major and even minor Palestinian Authority installations, including police stations, offices, security bases of all types, and intensified assassinations of activists. Some were known leaders.

Mustafa al-Zibri, better known as Abu Ali Mustafa, the leader of the Popular Front for the Liberation of Palestine, succeeded the beloved and well respected Dr. George Habash, the founder and leader of the PFLP. Abu Ali had come back into the West Bank in late 1999 after a few years of objecting to the Oslo Accords. He was greeted in many cities and towns. The PFLP, despite its smaller base of supporters, maintained respect for being a genuine independent Palestinian movement. I had met Abu Ali at a friend's apartment in Ramallah months before the Second Intifada. We both were invited to a private dinner. There were three other friends attending who were bankers and not interested in politics. I sat next to Abu Ali and reminded him of our meeting almost 19 years before in his Damascus office. We talked about the PLO, and I asked him about his outlook. He did not seem optimistic, but he spoke respectfully about Arafat. He said, "We meet, we talk, I demand PLO reform, he says of course, we agree on certain objectives to achieve, nothing happens, and that's Abu Ammar for you."

Abu Ali was accused by Israel of forming armed groups. Two Apache helicopters were involved in firing two rockets right through his office, which exploded inside and ended his life hardly a little over a year and a half after his return to Palestine. Abu Ali was never known for being a military leader. Most of his life was political and organizational. His death was a great loss. He was a voice of great conscience holding on to principles. He wanted peace, but for sure defined where the bottom line of compromise ended.

The PFLP never got enough credit for its influence on the PLO. It had always pushed for democracy, was a strong advocate of proportional representations through elections, and was a true representative system of popular vote for parties. Abu Ali Mustafa was assassinated on the 27th of August 2001. The PFLP did not wait long. On October 17, 2001, just about a month and a half later, it carried out the assassination of Rehavam Ze'evi, a minister in the Israeli government who was well-known for his extreme right-wing views of Palestinians. It was well orchestrated and shook the Israeli inner room of the political system. Israel continued to chase the PFLP activists who carried it out, as well as Ahmad Sa'adat, who succeeded Abu Ali Mustafa as the leader of the PFLP. He was held responsible for the assassination of Ze'evi and eventually kidnapped from a Palestinian Authority prison and imprisoned by Israel.

Oslo Accords Falling Apart

Sharon sent clear messages to Arafat that the rules of the game had changed. Sharon did not respect the Oslo Accords, or any of the agreements with the PLO and the Palestinian Authority. Any security threat to Israel was enough excuse for the IDF to penetrate into Area "A," which was supposed to be under the full security control of the PA. The IDF invaded one town after another, until they finally carried out an all-out reinvasion of all Palestinian Authority-controlled areas, including all major cities, towns, and villages.

On March 29, 2002, Ramallah was under a full-scale attack by the IDF. I was in my apartment in the middle of Ramallah, when suddenly, loud helicopters in the sky fired rockets, while Mirkava tanks roared into the streets, and sounds of nonstop heavy machine-gun fire erupted. The IDF faced mostly young Palestinian unprofessional fighters, firing their Kalashnikov automatic rifles, many of whom were killed and others were injured. These young men were extremely courageous to stand up in defense of Palestine and their leader Yasser Arafat, whose compound was fully encircled by IDF tanks and soldiers. The invasion was named by Israel "Operation Defensive Shield."

Evacuated by Marines

I felt very vulnerable in the apartment tower, then called some friends. I heard IDF soldiers were busting apartment doors, had their sniffing attack dogs with them, and harassed residents. I talked to Rakan, a good friend, who informed me what had happened to him when IDF soldiers arrived at his apartment. Not only did they wreck his place searching, they also forcibly took him out of his home and kept him in front when they busted into empty apartments, then they pushed him back inside and unleashed their dogs which attacked him. The process was repeated a couple of times until he collapsed, passed out, and was sent to a hospital. I could not bear the thought of just waiting until IDF soldiers showed up on my doorstep, but at the same time, I could not leave and go anywhere. Ramallah was a war zone. Many people were killed on the streets, and there was nowhere to go.

I then called the American Embassy and informed them of my desire to be evacuated out of Ramallah. The lady on the other end told me the embassy had no evacuation plans at that time, and that she would let me know as soon as one was prepared. She asked me other questions, most important was if I had any other citizenship or passport, and said if I did, especially Palestinian, Jordanian, or Israeli, that would have disqualified me for evacuation.

The next day I received a phone call from the same lady. She said, "You have 45 minutes. Someone will be coming to get you. His name is Jaber, and you can only bring a suitcase you can place on your lap."

Shortly after, Jaber called me and asked me to walk out of the apartment building and meet him at another location. I said there was no way I was going to walk anywhere. Snipers were shooting all over the place. I told him that if he was unable to come in front of the apartment building, I would rather stay. Jaber was quick to tell me to stay on the phone and give him directions, then he asked me to go down in front of the building where there would be two Suburban vehicles and to get into the second one. I rushed down.

As soon as I approached the second Suburban, the rear passenger door opened and a tall marine with a submachine gun and fully geared for battle appeared and put his hand against my chest in a stopping gesture. He searched me, then my little suitcase, and waved for me to get in the middle. Another marine was already in the backseat, one sat in front, and one was the driver. The two Suburbans moved forward. The marine in the front passenger seat was in constant communication describing all the details of the vehicle's location. He would even say, "We are turning. On our right a large trash container. We are next to a two-story building." We then passed by Arafat's compound. There were no shootings close by. I had the feeling the American Embassy informed both the Palestinians and the IDF of the evacuation and got their commitment for a secure route. A minute later, the marine on my side said, "You seem astonished." I answered, "I was expecting Jaber, not a couple of Rambos to come get me." He said, "There are 15 more Rambos in three more Suburbans waiting for us right at the Ramallah border." I was even more astonished, and totally shocked, when I asked, "How many people are you guys evacuating out of Ramallah with me?" He replied, "You are it."

Soon we arrived at the Ramallah border. The three other Suburbans joined us and the caravan moved on the road to Jerusalem. I said, "Wow, I feel like I'm President Clinton." The marine answered, "That's what we are here for." They dropped me off at the Ambassador Hotel where I wanted to be, and before they left, I asked them to come by when off duty for a beer. They said they would be happy to. The very next day, I was at the airport heading back to San Diego. I never saw those marines again, however, that moment was the first time in my life as an American citizen that I felt belonging to a country that cared about its people was wonderful. I felt that I owed those marines a great deal for taking such a risk to secure some man working in Ramallah, someone they never met and knew nothing about. I was deeply touched and sincerely appreciative.

I left Ramallah many times before and went back. Leaving Ramallah that time felt like no other, however. I realized the Oslo agreement and all other subsequent agreements collapsed. All Palestinian areas were again under full occupation, Arafat and most Palestinian leaders who supported and followed him as well as those who opposed the Oslo Accords were convinced the conflict with Israel took a historical strategic turn against prospects of peace. Arafat was put under an undeclared house arrest. He could not step out of his compound (the Mukataa). Even his compound was under gunfire. He moved from his office to other rooms, surrounded by his bodyguards. Despite the horrible siege and constant pressure, he portrayed tremendous courage and was a historic leader living his last days. He was offered the opportunity to go in exile again, however, instead, he went on Al Jazeera news in a live telephone interview and announced, "They want me murdered, jailed, or exiled, and I tell them I will only be a martyr."

In the last few months of his life, Arafat was loved the most and supported by the majority of his people. Even those who viciously opposed him for years found themselves supporting him. His refusal to bow down and give up on historic rights at the expense of his own life earned him a glorified status. There were times when the Mukataa was under heavy Israeli gunfire. Scores of Palestinians watching live television coverage of the attack went out on the streets of Ramallah—men, women, and youngsters marched to his compound shouting, "Abu Ammar, we protect you with our souls and our blood."

I spent 2 months back in California before I went back to Ramallah, and that time was just to wrap up and end my tenure and end my involvement with the Palestine Mortgage and Housing Corporation. When I was back a truce was in place, but it was very fragile. American mediations continued to try to make it hold, however, Ramallah seemed like it lost a good part of its soul. Streets were empty right before dark, and the project I most cared about seemed to be at stagnation. I did not see it going anywhere from there. I was very agitated, being pulled by my family in California and my job in Ramallah. I had to make a choice and decided to end my commitment and head back home.

Up Close and Personal within the Big Money Game

It was a few months after I returned to the U.S before I was offered an opportunity to join the newly formed Palestine Investment Fund, an investment company model which was meant to be similar to what is known as a sovereign investment fund. Similar to funds in many countries, it aimed to promote and support growth of the private sector through participating in companies and projects with an entrance-and-exit strategy. It was also supposed to invest domestically and abroad in friendly countries, as well as to maximize return on invested capital. The idea of setting up such a fund looked great on the surface, however, the undeclared objective of its founding was meant to limit Arafat's control and therefore his use of relatively large amounts of funds. It was to weaken what was viewed by the U.S. and Israel as his "mischief," and his undeclared new confrontational agenda after the failure of peace talks at Camp David.

I was invited to fly to London and meet a very controversial figure within the Palestinian political and economic system. His name Muayyad Mushid. He was known as Arafat's economic adviser . . . precisely, Arafat's moneyman. Although I met him a few times before, only once was it a long formal meeting. The other times were just greetings and exchanges of cordial words. A mutual friend suggested me to lead a professional technical team and contribute to institutionalize the newly founded Palestine Investment Fund (PIF), which was to acquire all investment holdings of a company named Palestine Commercial Services Company (PCSC), a company set up by Arafat and Muayyad Mushid and was totally run by Mushid. My trip to London and back was for a quick 48 hours. I met Mohammed, and we got to know each other more.

Our common friend conveyed to Mohammed the main terms I requested to take the job; thereafter I was hired as the deputy general manager and chief operating officer of the PIF.

Less than a month later, I left for Cairo where the head office of the fund was located. Mohammed was very unusual about the way he conducted business activities. He seemed to have classified his relationships with everyone he dealt with and behaved with them accordingly. He struck me as a very smart man, who found his way to power and money. He became close to people of great importance within Fatah and gained their confidence.

Mohammed is not Palestinian by origin. He is Kurdish Iraqi. He first joined a leftist Palestinian faction, became a journalist which introduced him to PLO leaders including Khalil Wazir "Abu Jihad," a military commander and well respected founding leader of Fatah. Thereafter, Mohammed met and got closer to Arafat himself.

Mushid was a charming and witty person. He knew how to use his charm when he needed to. I have also seen his other side, which was brutal. He worked closely with Arafat. His official title was the president's economic advisor, and in reality, he was involved with as much politics as economics and business. He had a large number of people on payroll, whether salaried employees of PCSC or simply the world-famous title of paying someone as a "consultant." Mushid was also a close ally of Mohammed Dahlan, former security chief of Gaza and longtime Fatah leading cadre who rose to power drastically after the Oslo agreement. Mushid was linked to action and decisions which warranted frequent negative publicity.

I took the job knowing his background. We obviously had very different views. However, I never believed differences with the head of any Palestinian institution should have kept anyone qualified from working for that institution. I strongly believed those institutions belonged to the Palestinian people. Many of my friends disagreed with me and surely would have stayed away if they were in my place. But I thought, on the contrary, by not engaging, we contributed to turning institutions into more of a closed circuit box, concentrating power in the hands of the few.

Associating with highly controversial people is not easy, and working with them is even harder. The intention was to have a professional team and a professional image, but our team was restricted with very limited authority. Even my efforts to set up an organizational chart with roles, responsibilities, and authority were to no avail. My actions were undermined, mostly by prolonging the matter endlessly. We were successful though in creating and implementing an investment decision-making system, which started with the investment management team and went on to the board of directors. The process was welcomed in the beginning and adopted. It worked and constantly recommended to the board of directors whether to approve new investments or dispose of existing ones. However, taking the institution building too seriously became a cause of unspoken tension between the old and the new way of doing business. I could imagine that at times Mushid most likely wished he never brought me in; on the other hand, once more, I thought I could contribute to building a true professional, transparent institution within an environment where favoritism and corruption were deeply rooted. It was said many times that I was acting like a "naïve American." In other words, out of touch with the reality surrounding me. To a great extent, I probably was. With my work, I earned the respect of many, however.

I did not gain enough support to be considered a permanent member of the inside circles of the Palestinian Authority. The reward would have been significant . . . a great deal of prestige and financial security. But the price, though, was too high. One would have had to become a stooge, surrender independence, and just follow instructions with no questioning from the major players of the cliques who controlled the PA, the ones who were able to place their loyal members in high places despite lacking the proper qualifications. To them, I seemed to have been a man who parachuted in, but remained a loose cannon—no one wanted to have me too close. They liked my work and capabilities to achieve goals for the public good; however, on the other hand, I was not loyal or obedient to the people in power. That was what they most cared to have and strongly demanded. I was diplomatic and tried so hard not to be confrontational, but it did not work. I was pushed to the limits where I had to draw a line; if I had not, I believe I would have sold out everything I stood for in my life, sold out the Palestinian cause as I saw it and believed in it, sold out the genuine people who paid a dear price for defending it and those who continue to suffer for it.

Institution building within the PLO and the Palestinian Authority was an illusion; power and private agendas of groups, and subagendas of individuals within those groups almost fully reflect the function of the entire Palestinian Authority. The PA turned out to be a political and economic body which consumed the Palestinian energy. It diverted the attention of most Fatah activists from the main goal of fighting for the historic cause of Palestine, to their own personal benefits. It had become a place where many personal empires of business and power were built, while others within the grassroots movement of Fatah and other factions still genuinely believed in the struggle for the cause of Palestine.

Money was made for the fund, and money was lost. Several times I was pushed hard to make bad recommendations. I did not, and was even worried most of that time to unintentionally make a bad recommendation. Some investment opportunities looked good on the surface, but once due diligence was made, major flaws appeared, and in the process of turning them down, I encountered severe pressure.

Arafat died on November 11, 2004. Mushid had spoken to me about his intention to leave the fund as early as 2 months after my joining. However, he stayed on upon Arafat's death, although he was preparing to leave. Mushid realized that he lost a huge protector, the highest authority of the PA. All indications were pointed to Mahmoud Abbas as a successor to Arafat, and given Mushid's sour relationship with Abbas, it was more logical for him to peacefully exit from the fund. His position in the fund came back to haunt him, however, when claims of corruption, fraudulent transactions, possible embezzlement, and money swindling were brought against him and two of his close confidants. They were indicted and received years of prison sentences and also ordered to pay millions of dollars to compensate for what was considered money they benefited from illegally during their work for the PIF. Last I checked, the three of them remain wanted by the Palestinian Authority.

I was phasing out of the PIF and happened to be in the U.S. when Mushid resigned. He had turned interim management over to his fully entrusted confidant. A few weeks later while I was in California, I received an e-mail from a World Bank Palestinian executive I had met only once before. I had no idea why he asked to talk to me. I called him, and to my surprise, he informed me President Abbas asked him to become the new general manager of the PIF, as well as his economic advisor. He had done some research and found out that Mushid had started his own investment company and took many staff members with him. He did not know how to start. I told him to look at it as an opportunity to restructure the PIF, and that many staff members were redundant. I volunteered and helped him get more familiar with the PIF management structure. I even convinced one of my previous team members to join him. I believed someone with his background was a good choice for transition.

Arafat, the Last Farewell, End of an Era

Chapter 19

After Arafat, Oslo No More, One State is the Only Solution

Arafat was viewed as responsible for starting the Second Intifada, and much more serious was his secret support of armed groups within Fatah . . . while looking the other way as other groups, like Hamas, were arming their paramilitary factions and conducted attacks on Israel. Arafat's refusal of Clinton's peace proposal was one big sin in the American administration's eyes. It marked the beginning of the end of American recognition of him. His support of the armed groups was enough for Sharon and others to push for, and possibly implement, his assassination. I was told many times by people who attended closed meetings with Arafat that he was blunt about his support for armed groups. It was no so secret. He did not announce it in the media, however, he spoke many times of his belief that Palestinians can't be unarmed and obtain a relatively just peace settlement with Israel.

Israel and other states involved in the Palestinian-Israeli conflict used the PA system they helped create to obtain compromises at the expense of the Palestinian cause. The PA became an environment where even people who did not own personal business empires but merely worked for the PA have a stake in it to maintain it as it was set up, for it had turned into their source of relative financial security.

Personal and group special interests created by the establishment of the PA became stronger than Arafat himself. During his last year, he was confined to his headquarters at the Mukataa in Ramallah. I had witnessed his power weaken by the day. I even heard some of those used to be his very close aides and advisors make jokes of what they claimed was "Arafat's disconnect with reality," and that "his stubbornness was keeping his thoughts contained within the ruins of his Mukataa." Others were more aggressive and worked on chipping away the authority of the historic leader. In the end, he fell mysteriously ill. The illness was widely believed to be caused by poison.

Arafat, the Last Farewell

The end of an era was sealed with his death. His last trip out of Ramallah was on a helicopter. People came out by the thousands to wish him farewell. Most of them knew he was not coming back alive, and he did not. He died in a French hospital. He was honored by a funeral ceremony in Paris that was fit for a king, then his body was flown to Egypt, where another funeral ceremony was held, with many presidents and world leaders in attendance. From there, his body was sent back to Ramallah, where thousands surrounded the helicopter which carried his body. It was a very emotional event. He was a leader beloved by most of his people. He was buried on the grounds of his Mukataa compound, although his desire was to have been buried in Jerusalem. Although Arafat disappeared from the Palestinian scene, his legacy remained.

Now a new course of Palestinian politics was set in motion. A more "moderate" compromising course, a term mostly used to induce a friendlier reaction with the U.S. and its allies. A new president and a prime minister came to power, more acceptable to the U.S., Israel, and even to moderate Arab states, which had abandoned Arafat in his last years.

Many years passed and more and more negotiations were held, but they did not yield freedom for Palestinians, nor did they liberate their lands or create an independent state. Billions of dollars more were poured into the West Bank, especially with a former International Monetary Fund (IMF) senior Palestinian executive, Salam Fayyad, as prime minister, and his publicized plans for future state institution building. He was trusted and well liked by the U.S. and Europe, however, his tenure ended sadly with a lot of blame aimed at him for economic problems, rising public debt, and a power struggle between him and Fatah.

Legitimacy and Democracy

Hamas, as a result of elections held in January 2006, had won the majority of seats of the Palestinian Legislative Council (PLC), the PA parliament. Abbas was forced by the election results to appoint Ismail Haniyeh, a Hamas leader, as prime minister. A power struggle between the two factions ended in armed clashes in Gaza. Hamas prevailed. After it overran Fatah's armed men and exerted full control of the Gaza strip, Abbas responded and fired the Hamas-named prime minister and appointed Fayyad. Haniyeh then refused to step down, and as a result, Palestinians ended up with a president, two prime ministers, and a parliament—with expired terms for all of them, yet they continued to rule. On the bright side, the United Nations General Assembly had, on November 29, 2012, voted and granted "Palestine" a nonmember observer status, which sounds great and gives Palestinians access and more legitimacy to many United Nations agencies.

Reality

The situation on the ground remains the same. The Palestinian people in Gaza live in poor, densely populated neighborhoods. People in the West Bank have two security forces policing them—their own PA on one side, and the IDF on the other. They have no freedom of movement and no certain future. Living expenses are skyrocketing. Nothing has changed for the inhabitants of its refugee camps, those who came to the West Bank from pre-1948 Palestine. Palestinian citizens of Israel, struggle separately for their rights and national heritage, and worst of all, Palestinians in Lebanese refugee camps live in a small, confined geography with almost no hope of a better future.

In Syria, Palestinians are caught in the middle of a civil war. Jordan and the rest of the Diaspora continue to wait for a solution which would reconnect them together as a people and bond them with their homeland. The greatest majority of the Palestinian people did not, and will not, relinquish their right to their historic homeland in historical Palestine. They proved it through many ruthless years, relocating refugees, improving their economic conditions, and providing them with citizenships in other countries—and it did not make them dissolve and disappear. What happened to the Palestinians ranks amongst some of the biggest events of the twentieth century.

Meanwhile, Israel continues to build more settlements, with over half a million settlers scattered throughout the West Bank. Israeli governments continue the strategy of engaging in endless, fruitless negotiations with Palestinian interlocutors. We are no closer to seeing a final settlement or permanent solution to the problem. Israelis don't want to give up the West Bank and Gaza. They would very much like to get rid of the Palestinians inhabiting them, and even discard the

Palestinian Israelis if they could. One thing is certain: Two people are living on the same historic land of Palestine. The one can't, and will not be able to, deny the other, which leads to the realization that whether we like it or not, we can—and must—accept each other. There are two things we must get rid of, and they are racism and discrimination, both religious and ethnic. If we believe in human and citizenship equality, we can all live together in a just and democratic society, Palestinian and Israeli . . . Muslim, Jewish, and Christian in one country and one state ruled by the people with one man, one vote, and fair representation of all.

Zionist Israelis believe this would contradict Herzl's vision of a Jewish state; some Palestinians would consider it a sellout of historic rights. The fact remains, however, aside from ideological and religious beliefs, nothing should prevent Palestinian and Jewish people from building one state. Why not? It is possible if it would be founded on the solid foundations of freedom, justice, and democracy for all.

Made in the USA
Las Vegas, NV
23 October 2023